Maksim Asenov

COURAGE IN CRISIS

The Ultimate Guide to Success

To Paul and Claire with much love From Nikolay and Yordanka

SM
SIGNATURE.
message

28 27 26 25 24 23   9 8 7 6 5 4 3 2 1

COURAGE IN CRISIS: The Ultimate Guide to Success

Copyright ©2023 Maksim Asenov

All rights reserved. Except as permitted under the U.S. Copyright Act of 1976, no part of this publication may be reproduced, distributed, or transmitted in any form by any means, or stored in a database or retrieval system, without the prior written permission of the author and/or publisher. Printed in the United States.

Published by:
Signature Message, llc
17450 Bramble Court Yorba Linda, CA 92886

Library of Congress Cataloging-in-Publication Data:
ISBN: 979-8-376975-83-1
E-book available exclusively from Amazon in Kindle Format

BISAC:
SEL027000   SELF-HELP / Personal Growth / Success
REL012090   RELIGION / Christian Living / Professional Growth

CONTENTS

Foreword 1

Introduction 3

PART ONE It's Time To Find Your 'Why' 11

Chapter 1   Finding Your Purpose 13

Chapter 2   Anatomy of Success 26

Chapter 3   Success Is a Choice…Literally 42

PART TWO It Starts With First Principles 55

Chapter 4   The First Principle of Faith 57

Chapter 5   The First Principle of Action 72

Chapter 6   First Principle of Courage 86

PART THREE Discovering Your Inner Power 103

Chapter 7   The Power of Pressure 105

Chapter 8   The Power Of Identity 120

Chapter 9   The Power of Habits 136

Chapter 10   No Turning Back Now 155

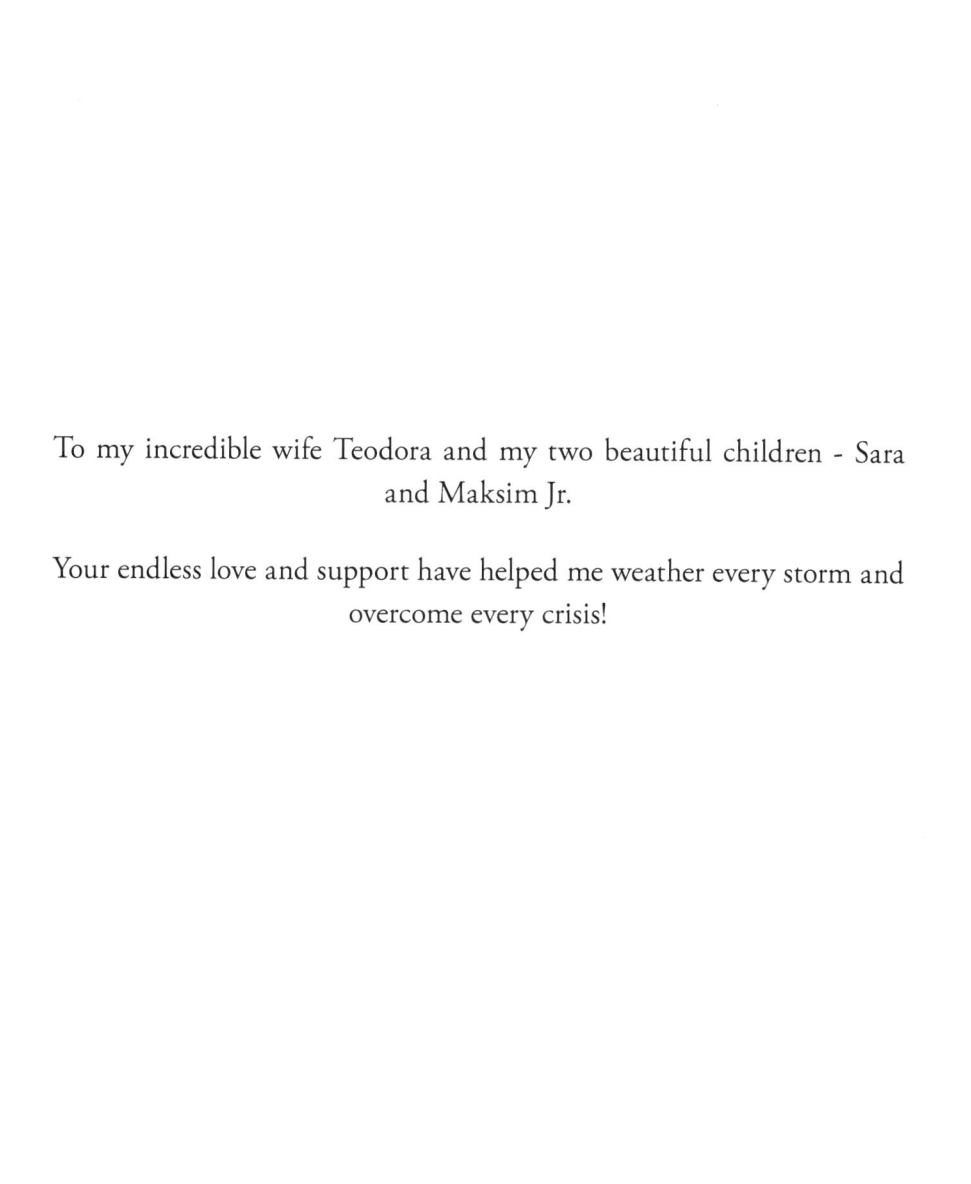

To my incredible wife Teodora and my two beautiful children - Sara and Maksim Jr.

Your endless love and support have helped me weather every storm and overcome every crisis!

FOREWORD

By Tim Storey

As I have had the privilege of knowing Maksim Asenov and his ministry for several years, I have been continually impressed by his deep compassion for others and his unique ability to connect with people from all walks of life. Maksim is truly a master at inspiring and motivating others to reach their full potential.

In today's world, it is all too easy to become overwhelmed by fear and uncertainty. However, Maksim's new book, Courage in Crisis: The Ultimate Guide to Success, offers a beacon of hope for anyone facing difficult times. Through his powerful and practical guidance, Maksim empowers readers to find their own courage and overcome the obstacles that stand in their way.

I wholeheartedly recommend this book to anyone seeking to navigate life's challenges with grace and resilience. Maksim's wisdom and insights will inspire you to rise above your fears and achieve success in every area of your life.

INTRODUCTION
Your Crisis Playbook

Every life story has immense value, and if one could learn to extract the lessons from the legacy of the past, it becomes a recipe for future success. More than that, it helps you create meaning out of your otherwise meaningless suffering. In the midst of great pain, however, it is often hard to see beyond the current circumstances, and it's only natural to wonder, "Why is this happening to me?".

What if you had someone to help you ask the right questions? You will arrive at some inspiring and life-transformational conclusions. Maybe this is why life coaches are one of the highest-paid professions in the world today—they help you extract meaning, create a plan and be strategic in your actions. And that is why I wrote this book and called it "Courage in Crisis." This is my endeavor to support you through your journey as I wish someone had done for me.

Since the start of my coaching and speaking career, I've taught about the meaning of life—my life, your life, human life, animal and yes—even plant life—life on this planet is something so fascinating yet full of pain and crisis. And maybe this is the reason why it is so interesting and meaningful. Maybe the challenges and difficulties are exactly what makes life worth living. The true question is not if you will encounter a crisis but rather, are you prepared for it? Do you have a strategy for how to deal with it when it strikes?

When you find yourself in a crisis, it's easy to feel shaken, discouraged, and powerless. Struggle has an uncanny ability to make us feel unable, unstable, and uncertain about ourselves and our future.

There are big and small crises, personal and communal ones, and the way we deal with them determines not just what we achieve but, in a very real sense, who we are. That said, there can be no real courage without a crisis. It is the only context in which you can be courageous, become a hero, and accomplish something real and meaningful. There can be no hero without adversity, good without evil, crown without a cross, and resurrection without death.

It begins With a Crisis

Growing up in one of the largest and most dangerous ghettos in Eastern Europe, I lived in a state of permanent crisis. To say my mother and I were poor would be a significant understatement of our genuinely dire circumstances. Daily struggles, such as not knowing when our next meal would be or how we would afford even the most basic necessities, were the norm. My greatest hero was my grandma, a single mother and self-made entrepreneur who, through sheer willpower and hard work, managed to build a home and raise her three children all by herself. I was just twelve when I saw her pass away in my mother's arms. From that moment on our family began to fall apart.

My uncle became increasingly dependent on alcohol, my aunt fell deeper into depression, and my mother found herself in an abusive relationship that almost cost her her life. This crisis lasted for roughly two years. I can still remember hearing my mother cry herself to sleep every night as we moved from house to house, trying to escape the threats of her abusive ex-boyfriend. Not long after she fled to Greece, leaving me alone to live in a house with no electricity or running water in the darkness of winter.

Why I Wrote This Book

Despite the pain and suffering I experienced, I have come to understand the value of crisis. When things fall apart, they create opportunities to re-think, re-adjust, and re-imagine your life, who you can be, and what you can achieve.

Ever since I was a little boy, I have spent my life learning, applying, and refining a set of principles that would eventually take me far away from the broken home of my youth and become the foundation of my success in life, family, and career.

Today, my life looks very different from the crisis I grew up in. I am a happily married man, a father of two beautiful children, the Lead Pastor of the fastest-growing church in Bulgaria, and the CEO of one of the nation's largest and most successful executive coaching companies. However, when I reflect deeply on my life, I realize that I wouldn't be the person I am today if it weren't for the suffering I went through.

In this book, I share some of the most valuable lessons and stories from my journey and ultimately answer the question—how did I transition from a boy with no apparent future to becoming the successful man I am today. Despite all my successes, my greatest accomplishment has been maintaining my integrity and values throughout my journey. I have learned that without a strategic approach, we risk selling ourselves short and becoming a public success but a private failure. I once believed it was impossible to have a fulfilling family life, lead a church, build a business, and be a good father all at the same time. But, with courage and determination, I have been able to prove otherwise. My family, including my wife Teodora, our two children, and the hundreds of spiritual children we have mentored, are living proof that we can exchange a life of misery and instability for one of success and prosperity. And the key to that is how we handle crises.

There is a set of proven principles that I learned in my most difficult moments that can encourage you to overcome your greatest challenges and make it through your turbulent storms. These principles are the contents of this book. If you can learn, apply and master them, you will not only discover how to get through any crisis life throws at you, but you will also unlock a level of success so remarkable and unimaginable that it will change your life and the lives of your children's children too.

It's Time To Find Your Courage

It was the writer Anais Nin who said, *"Life shrinks or expands in proportion to one's courage."* When you are feeling the fear of a crisis, it's easy to cower, avoid, and evade it. When faced with the giant of fear, courage will give you the strength to defeat even your greatest enemy.

> *Courage is the ability to do something that frightens one. Having strength in the face of pain or grief.*

If you want to make it through the crisis you're in, you need courage–lots of it. You need to be brave and willing enough to confront the fear you feel and the pain you are in. You need to have the fortitude to lean forward at the exact moment you want to jump. Despite how tough the battle is, you must never give up, never give in, and never surrender. You must have incredible courage in the midst of an unprecedented crisis. If you do, you can overcome any challenge and climb any mountain between you and your dreams.

When Crisis Strikes

I finished the first draft of this book In early 2020. It was a project that took me roughly eight months to complete. Yet, it felt like a lifetime. For as long as I can remember, I have been obsessed with the question, "What was it that made people successful?" How, despite great challenges and unprecedented crises, some people are still able to achieve remarkable success in their life, family, and business?

Within days of sending my manuscript to my editor, it seemed as if the whole world had turned upside down. News agencies began flooding the airways with reports of global virus outbreaks. Suddenly, the future of everything became uncertain.

Covid-19 changed everything for me, my church, and my coaching team. Within one week of the initial global hysteria, both Awakening church and my Executive coaching business were completely shut down and barred from holding public events or meetings in person. My annual speaking schedule, which included several dozen planned speaking events, was all canceled within a few days. Conferences and seminars my team and I invested massive amounts of time, money, and creative energy were postponed indefinitely.

As a spiritual leader and business owner, I knew the organizations I was responsible for were in the midst of a crisis. For as long as I can remember, crises have been a part of my life. Despite the uniqueness of the situation, I knew the lessons I had learned in the past would still apply to the present. This was the perfect opportunity to apply the principles I had just compiled within this book and re-test them under unprecedented circumstances.

That's exactly what I did, and the results were extraordinary.

The Power of Courage In Crisis

On the second day of lockdown, I texted the team leaders from my various organizations to join me on a zoom call where I explained that despite the precariousness of the current situation, we had an incredible opportunity in front of us. While most people would spend their time caught up in the crisis, we would spend our time serving the missions of our organizations. I assured them that if we worked as a team and used our creative skills and resources to rise to the occasion, we would survive and thrive. Over the next two years, that is exactly what happened.

We switched from live services to broadcasting exclusively online within a few days. Quickly, our new online Sunday Experiences became a huge success. It turned out that preaching online had a few previously unknown advantages. I extended my teaching time and reached many more people who lived outside our church's typical reach. As a church, we also found creative ways to serve and support people who were quarantined and stuck in their homes. We started a food drive that distributed tons of groceries to poor and socially disadvantaged families around our city. We paid rent for others who had lost their jobs so they would not be evicted. We covered utility bills for families with children so they could keep the lights and hot water on.

During the entire course of the pandemic, neither the church nor my business lost money. Instead, the opposite happened. We grew exponentially. New online attendees meant that people who had never given to our church began to support our mission. My executive coaching business multiplied due to the increased demand of business leaders attempting to navigate Covid-19. Meanwhile, my personal net worth also tripled.

The same set of proven success principles I had used to build my life before Covid-19 also led to our team's success through it. The experience solidified in me the core thesis of this book—the greater the crisis, the greater the opportunity to achieve success.

Your Journey Ahead

I can personally guarantee that each one of my principles has been tested over many years. This book serves as a toolkit, a playbook of proven principles that can be used to confidently build the life you desire. It is not a magic pill. If you want to achieve lasting success, it requires full commitment and honesty about your current situation, your goals, and the steps necessary to achieve them. However, if you have the courage to do so, applying and mastering the principles in this book will make you unstoppable.

Imagine a life where each challenge leads to more success and better outcomes in the long run. Even when the path is uncertain, you always know the correct combination to open all the right doors and take the right actions to achieve the desired results every time. How different would your life be? How different would the lives of your loved ones be? How different would your financial and professional life be? It is possible to master the art of turning pressure into power, struggles into strength, and a desert into a wellspring. When you know the secret to using your toughest moments to your greatest advantage, you will be unstoppable and unbeatable in the game of life.

PART ONE

It's Time To Find Your 'Why'

It was the great German philosopher Friedrich Nietzsche who once said, "He who has a *why* to live for can bear almost any how." Nothing could be closer to the truth when finding courage in a crisis. When things get tough, it's easy to lose sight, lose focus, and ultimately lose your footing. What will keep you focused, determined, and always headed in the right direction is your north star. Your north star is your *why*.

Your *why* is what drives you. It's your dream. It's what you're aiming at and working for. It's what you desire most to do, be, and achieve. It's your purpose.

Your *why* is the most powerful weapon in your success toolkit. The stronger your *why* is, the more likely you are to push through adversity and keep going. If you know your *why*, your struggle will transform from *suffering* to *sacrifice*. Your pain will transition from meaningless to purposeful serving, and your setbacks will change from failures to lessons learned. That's what your why does. Despite how challenging life might get, your why will make it all worth it.

It's finally time to find your *why*.

CHAPTER ONE
Finding Your Purpose

"Knowing your life purpose is the first step toward living a truly conscious life. A life purpose provides us with a clear goal, a set finish line that you truly want to reach."
Simon Foster

I never knew my father. I was mainly raised by women. The only male role model I had was my uncle who did his best to support me. We were very poor and lived in the largest and most dangerous ghetto in Eastern Europe. When I was thirteen, my mother and I were on the run for over two years. We moved from house to house as we evaded her abusive ex-boyfriend. He had not only physically assaulted her but also threatened to kill her. Eventually my mother fled to Greece in an attempt to save her life. I was fifteen, left alone to live in a house with no electricity or running water.

The winter months in Bulgaria were brutal and unimaginably cold. The home I lived in was poorly insulated. My daily morning routine consisted of filling a bath with buckets of ice-cold water from a neighbor, in a house with no heating in the dead of winter. I walked to school at 26 degrees below zero temperatures.

One late night, after visiting a friend's house, I discovered that the main waste pipe had exploded and filled our entire house with indescribably odorous excrement and sewage. Despite my best efforts to literally shovel out the shit, there was too much waste to remove in one night. Completely defeated, I decided to shovel snow into the house instead to cover the massive amount of waste. Eventually, I created a narrow snow path from the front door all the way to my bed.

As I was lying in bed, trying to sleep, and surrounded by shit, I began to laugh out loud. In an attempt to bring levity to a truly horrible situation, I told myself, "This would make a great story one day." It was a moment I will never forget. That night, I decided right then and there that I would completely change my life. Despite the absolute misery of my upbringing, I knew there was more to life than the hardship and squalor that my mother and I endured daily. There had to be a different way to live, structure, and organize my life that would lead me down a different path and produce different outcomes. There had to be a way to exchange a life of misery and instability for one of success and prosperity. Whatever it was, I was going to find it. No matter how long it took or how many giants I had to slay to get there, this would not be my life. I was determined to take whatever actions were necessary to change my circumstances and alter my fate.

It Starts With Purpose

It was the great American writer Joseph Campbell who said, *"The dark night of the soul comes just before revelation."* It's often during our darkest moments and greatest challenges that we are inspired toward courageous action. When faced with a life-changing crisis, we have two choices: stay stuck or find a purpose big enough to inspire enough courage to lead us out of it. According to Collins dictionary, the definition of purpose is:

The reason for which something is done or created or for which something exists. It's your motivation, cause, and objective.

The most powerful force on earth is an individual brave enough to commit themselves to a greater purpose. You need a reason strong and big enough to get you back up after you have been knocked down. Despite the situation you are in, make a decision to relentlessly pursue what holds the most significance to you.

In my experience, there are one of two ways people discover their life's purpose, and they are often interrelated:

To Avoid A Destination - Pain and suffering are the most formidable forces in the world. At times, the most effective motivator is avoiding a dire outcome. Maybe you grew up in poverty and strongly desire to improve your circumstances. Maybe you have witnessed friends or loved ones battling addiction and are determined to make healthier choices. Knowing what you don't want or want to avoid can be just as important as knowing what you want.

To Realize A Vision - There is a well-known proverb that says, "Knowing is half the battle." This holds particularly true when it comes to life. If you want to be successful, you need to have a vision for your life and a destination you are choosing to travel to. The first step in discovering your purpose is creating a clear vision of what you want in life, who you want to be, and how you want to get there.

What Are You Aiming At?

I was fifteen years old and on my own. With little to no support, I had no idea how to build my life. Despite having no present positive role models to look up to and learn from, I knew that I wanted to be successful. The trouble was I didn't know any successful people. I would find myself openly wondering, 'How did they dress? Where did they spend their time? How did they live and organize themselves, their lives, and businesses?'

Every day after school and on weekends, I began to venture out of the ghetto I lived in and explored the nicest parts of town. I went to the most expensive restaurants and ordered the only thing I could afford, a cup of coffee, just to experience the atmosphere. I would browse designer stores even though I couldn't buy anything just to learn about high fashion. I listened to messages from leaders, public speakers, and pastors from all over the world and vigorously took extensive notes.

After I spent years exposing myself to as much education and observation as possible, I slowly but surely began understanding the nature of success. The first lesson I learned was a revelation that, at first, struck me like lightning. To be successful, I needed to have a clear target I was aiming at. That meant creating a vision for my life, deciding what success meant for me, and determining what I was willing to sacrifice to get there.

It Takes Great Purpose

It was former President of Disney–ABC Television Group Anne Sweeney who once said, "Define success on your own terms, achieve it by your own rules, and build a life you're proud to live." It can't be said any better than that. Success Principle #1 The first and fundamental principle of success is there is no single definition of success. Every person must develop their own personal definition.

As an executive coach, I have been privileged to coach exceptionally successful people: celebrities, CEO's, professional athletes, and entrepreneurs. They are all very different people with diverse stories, backgrounds, dreams, goals, and visions. All of them, however, have one thing in common: they are well on their way to achieving the life they want. What makes them all different are the targets they are aiming at. To put it differently, they are all successful in various ways.

Success is the accomplishment of an aim or purpose.

In that sense, success is directly related to your purpose. To quote Victor Frankl, author of the global best-selling book *Man's Search For Meaning*, "Life is never made unbearable by circumstances, but only by lack of meaning and purpose." You cannot have courage in crises without first having a vision that inspires courage. You cannot reach your goals unless you have the means to measure progress. You cannot achieve success unless you have an aim or purpose specific and meaningful enough to carry you through great struggle and significant sacrifice.

That is why you need an extraordinary vision. Having a vision is more than just having a desire or wish, it's a clear and detailed picture of your ideal future and the person you want to become. To truly succeed, it's important to define what success means to you and have the courage to stay true to your goals and values.

Discovering Your Life Areas

This book is based on three foundational principles. First, life is made up of eight interrelated domains. Achieving success in life encompasses more than just financial prosperity, professional accomplishments or excelling at work. Regardless of your personal definition of success, it will include some, if not all, of these eight Life Success Areas:

> **Area One | Career:** Your profession
> **Area Two | Finances:** Your personal and family finances
> **Area Three | Health:** Your physical health
> **Area Four | Spiritual:** Your connection to God
> **Area Five | Romance:** Your romantic relationships
> **Area Six | Family:** Your relationship with family members
> **Area Seven | Environment:** Your surroundings
> **Area Eight | Personal Growth:** Your intellectual or skill development

Second, every Life Area is important. Why? Because every Life Area is interconnected with each other. For instance, your career is directly connected to your finances. The better you perform professionally, the more money you will make. Your health, on the other hand, is connected to every area. All seven other areas might be directly or indirectly affected if you suffer from health problems. Having a definition of success that incorporates every life area goes a long way to achieving the level of success you desire.

You can improve any Life Area you desire. Whatever your score might be, I promise you can change it. I do not believe people are destined to repeat the past. You can change, adjust, and transform your life.

Third, the clearer your definition of success is, the more likely you are to reach it. Once you have given yourself your Life Area score, take a few moments to write down, in one to four sentences, what your ideal vision for that life area might be. For example, when you envision your future family, you might have a lot of children in a house full of love. When you imagine your career, you might see yourself as an entrepreneur who owns your own company. When you envision your finances, you might see yourself as debt-free, with a home paid off and plenty of retirement savings. The more specific you are about what you want, the more likely you are to achieve your goals.

LIFE SUCCESS AREAS

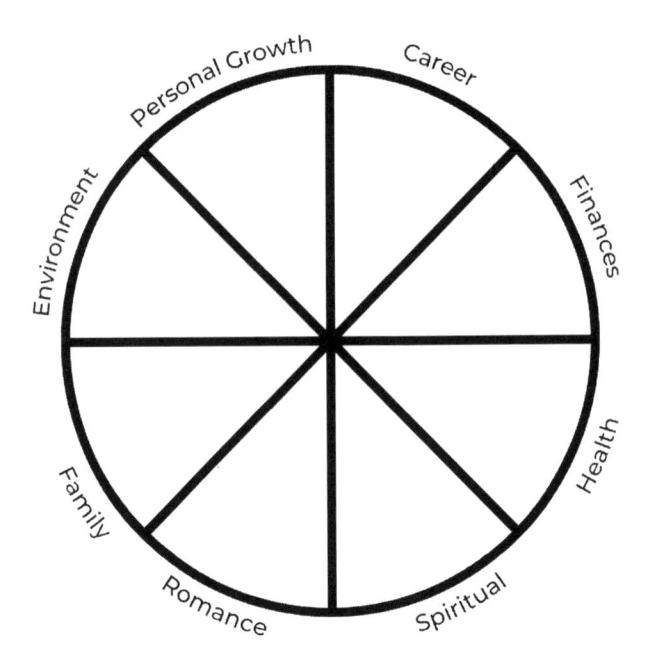

The *Life Success Areas Assessment* is the tool I use to help my clients identify areas of their lives they would like to improve. Use it to measure your progress towards your personal success goals within each area. If you haven't taken it yet, you can find the *Life Success Areas Assessment* at the end of this chapter! It will take you five to ten minutes to do. Best of all, it will provide you with an easy way to organize your personal success vision for your life.

It's Time To Dig Deep

I want to share with you a simple truth that will radically change your life. Every successful person alive today or in human history started from the same position you are in. Seriously. In his book The *Millionaire Next Door*, Thomas J. Stanley explains that more than 80% of American millionaires are first-generation "rich" or self-made.[1] That means that four out of five wealthy people started with nothing. Each one of them most likely felt insecure, struggled with feeling like they weren't good enough, and questioned if they could do it, be it, and reach it.

Self-doubt is a part of the journey from where you are to where you want to go. The key is not to let self-doubt hold you back. Instead, use it as a tool and a weapon to achieve your dreams. If you are unsure what you are capable of, let this be the moment you decide to find out. If you feel limited, make the decision to push yourself to the limit and see how far you can go.

That is what it means to have a vision. Your personal success vision should not be a description of what you can do. Instead, it should be a future picture of who you could be and what you could achieve. This is your moment to dream courageously and speak your heart's true desires. Here are three steps that will bring clarity to your dreams and empower you to realize them.

STEP ONE | Be Honest About What You Want

When you have struggled, lost, or been disappointed, it is easy to believe that great things cannot happen in the future, and even easier, to never

---

[1] Thomas J. Stanley, *The Millionaire Next Door* (Simon & Schuster, 1996) pg. 84.

strive toward your desires at all. I am convinced that the number one reason most people never reach their goals, realize their vision, and manifest their dreams is that they don't dare to speak honestly and openly about what they want.

Being honest about what you want can be scary and even painful. Why? Because you might not obtain it, you might not reach it, and you might fail and fail terribly. That's scary. It's so frightening it keeps most people on the sidelines, never willing to play and win in the game of life.

Hockey Hall of Famer Wayne Gretzky said, "You miss 100% of the shots you don't take." What is true in hockey is also true in life. Sure, you might miss some shots, and you might even make some pretty big mistakes and fail many times along the way. In fact, I can guarantee you will. But I can also assure you that the more honest you are with yourself about what you want and who you want to be, regardless of the distance between you and what you desire, the more likely you will be to manifest success.

STEP TWO | Learn From the Success of Others

When I was a teenager, I spent a lot of time studying successful people. In time, I tried to develop a personal vision for my life. The problem was that I had never encountered an individual who had achieved what I was passionate about in the way I wanted to achieve it. This meant that my internal picture of my desired future self was blurry. I felt extremely insecure when making significant decisions along my success journey. I would often feel scared and continually question myself and my internal reasoning. For example, if I decided to become a pastor, did that mean I couldn't own and grow a secular coaching business? If I was passionate about coaching business executives, could I still make a difference as a spiritual leader and humanitarian? For a tumultuous season, my inner contradictions created real outer conflict. My inability to merge these two visions of my future left me feeling empty, discouraged, and defeated. I openly wondered to myself and my wife if I could make it or if I should even try at all.

Everything changed when I discovered a man named Tim Storey. He was a preacher just like me, yet he was also a life coach and a humanitarian. For over forty years, he spiritually influenced millions of people in over seventy-five countries. Yet, he coached some of Hollywood's biggest stars and America's most prominent business leaders.

Right then, I decided to follow this man and learn everything I could from him. I studied the way he built his career, how he spoke about God, and how he approached life coaching. The more I learned, the less blurry the future of my life became and the less insecure I felt. The more I realized that what I wanted to do could be done, the more convinced I became I could do it.

That's exactly what happened. Eighteen years later, Tim Storey, the man who showed me that my dreams were possible, wrote the foreword to this book.

STEP THREE | Define Success for You
Writer Betty Friedan was right when she said, "You can have it all, just not all at once." The most common mistake people make at the beginning of their success journey is expecting to simultaneously achieve great success in every area of their lives. They believe they can have the perfect career, be the ideal parents, and still have enough time to go on vacation twice a year. Then, when they struggle to realize their success vision, they feel discouraged, depressed, and disillusioned. They waste months, years, and even decades striving after something they can never reach instead of spending the same energy enjoying the journey and the fruits of their labor.

Here is the truth. Every definition of success has its trade-offs. The reason is that time is a zero-sum game. That means when you spend time focusing on one area, you cannot focus on another. That is why it is essential to be honest with yourself about your priorities. An excellent exercise for identifying what you care about most is ranking your Life Areas in order of importance. If you know that having a family is more important to you than making a lot of money, be willing to spend more time with your kids and less time working. Suppose your definition of success means you care about the environment you live in. In that case, it might be worth focusing on financial planning so you can afford a bigger house in an affluent neighborhood. When defining success for yourself, there is no wrong answer. It is fully customizable. Your only limit is your imagination.

Defining Success for You

One of the most common problems I deal with as a coach is counseling people who recently realized they spent the last twenty to thirty years working towards a vision for their lives that was not truly theirs. Yes, they have achieved success, but it's "false success." Their life made them more empty and miserable. They sacrificed what they truly wanted in pursuit of a purpose that was not worth it in the end. It's the CEO who sacrificed his relationship with his family and his marriage, or the woman who gave up having children in the pursuit of a career she thought she wanted. It is the son who tried to please his parents by marrying a girl he did not love.

Life is the sum total of your choices, decisions, and sacrifices. To truly achieve the success you desire, you must be brave enough to create your own vision, live your own purpose, and pursue your own dream.

Begin the process of building your success pathway by taking inventory of the eight life areas in the *Life Success Areas Assessment*. Use it as a catalyst to jumpstart your success journey and keep track of your progress as you move towards your most important goals.

CHAPTER 1
PRINCIPLES

Success Principle #1
Commit to a greater purpose.

Success Principle #2
Discover your eight Life Success Areas.

Success Principle #3
Be honest about what you want.

Success Principle #4
Learn from the success of others.

Success Principle #5
Define success for you.

Chapter 1 Exercise
EXAMPLE | YOUR LIFE AREAS

Each of our lives is a sum total of eight interconnected life areas.

Rate yourself from 1-10 in each life area.

SUCCESS LIFE AREAS	SCALE	SCORE
CAREER	1-10	8
FINANCE	1-10	9
HEALTH	1-10	7
SPIRITUAL	1-10	5
ROMANCE	1-10	6
FAMILY	1-10	9
ENVIRONMENT	1-10	8
PERSONAL GROWTH	1-10	4

QUESTIONS:

1. What 1-3 areas are you currently most succeeding in?

   I have a great career, making my ideal salary, and I am very involved in my church.

2. What 1-3 areas would you like to improve in the next 12 months?

   I am 40 pounds overweight. Long hours at work limit my social life. I also want to spend more quality time with my wife and kids.

Chapter 1 Exercise
YOUR LIFE AREAS

Each of our lives is a sum total of eight interconnected life areas.
Rate yourself from 1-10 in each life area.

SUCCESS LIFE AREAS	SCALE	SCORE
CAREER	1-10	
FINANCE	1-10	
HEALTH	1-10	
SPIRITUAL	1-10	
ROMANCE	1-10	
FAMILY	1-10	
ENVIRONMENT	1-10	
PERSONAL GROWTH	1-10	

QUESTIONS:

1. What 1-3 areas are you currently most succeeding in?

2. What 1-3 areas would you like to improve in the next 12 months?

CHAPTER TWO
Anatomy of Success

"Be the change you want to see in the world."
Mahatma Gandhi

Of all nature's creatures, butterflies are some of the most beautiful ones. The vibrant colors and beautiful patterns that decorate their wings make them stand out everywhere they are. Some species even have sparkling blue wings so bright that pilots can spot them from above. It is hard to imagine that every butterfly began its journey as a lowly caterpillar—an insect that could not be more different in almost every way. Butterflies soar freely through the air, whereas caterpillars inch along the ground. Butterflies have small, fragile bodies and a set of giant wings. Caterpillars are long, plump, and husky. Yet, through the process of metamorphosis, every caterpillar has the potential to become a majestic butterfly.

Even within nature itself, there is an anatomy of success. There is a proven path to transforming your inner potential into outer beauty. There is a method to transform the crisis you are facing into a gateway to success.

It Starts With a Metanoia

The ancient Greeks had a word they used to describe a person who experienced a remarkable transformation in their life. It was called Metanoia. Metanoia means the journey of changing one's mind, heart, self, or way of life. Many writers would even describe it as an inner spiritual conversion. To experience metanoia meant encountering a personal truth, a religious revelation, or an experience of purpose that was so real and powerful that it would turn their life upside down and inside out. They would be inspired and empowered to reorient themselves completely, which means changing how they thought, spoke, acted, and lived. That is Metanoia.

You need to experience your own Metanoia, and come to a place where you are convinced that personal transformation is your only way forward. You must know with all your heart, might, and soul that the way you are living right now will not get you to where you want to go. You have to accept that your current behaviors cannot be your future ones. Come to terms with the decisions that got you here in order to discover what you can do to move forward.

To experience Metanoia will take courage. Lots of courage. But you have it in you. If you are willing to be honest with yourself, face your greatest fears, and fight for a Metanoia, you will unlock the door to true transformation.

It's Time To Be Honest

For Most of my life I was overweight. For years, I felt tired and depressed. I was stuck in a pattern of excuses, regret, and denial. When my wife and I founded Awakening Church, we worked long hours and never took days off. Due to all that stress, lack of self-care, and meals at odd hours my weight increased even further reaching 250 pounds. All that extra weight determined how I looked and felt about myself. Every day, my personal feelings of failure, inadequacy, and insecurity hung over me like a dark cloud.

Self-conscious about my midsection, I began to look for affirmation from people close to me. Every Sunday before I got on stage, I would nervously ask my wife, "How do I look?" Always loving and supportive, she would say with a smile, "Handsome." After my messages, I would self-consciously ask the production crew the same question, "How did I look on stage today?" They would enthusiastically respond, "You looked great!"

For months, I accepted their words. "If I look okay," I thought, "I guess I am okay!" With little to no incentive to change, I continued to perform the same habits and behaviors that led to my present body weight. As time went on, my physical and mental health continued to deteriorate. My outer tiredness and inner feelings of depression and insecurity got even worse.

Then one morning, while on a trip to Israel, I visited the Wailing Wall to pray for my church, family, and future. As I reflected on my life, I heard an inner voice speak a hidden truth. I was hurting myself. My poor health had the potential to rob me of the future I knew I was called to live. Holding back tears, I knew my life was too important to let myself go. People who needed my help were waiting for me on the other side of my commitment to transform my life and health.

Shortly after returning to Bulgaria, I shared my experience with the editor of my first book. Seeing the seriousness in my eyes, she quickly recommended a health specialist and personal trainer. It didn't take long before I booked my initial consultation.

After performing a physical examination and receiving my lab results, he sat me down in his office. "How am I doing, doc? It's not so bad, right?" I asked nervously. He replied sternly, "Maksim, you are really doing badly. Even though you are only twenty-five years old, you have the metabolic age of someone in their fifties."

As he spoke, I was completely taken aback. For months, I had been telling myself that I was okay! Despite the reality I faced in the mirror, I had continued to use high-carbohydrate foods as an emotional crutch.

My denial made me ignore the harm I was causing myself without ever making any changes. The longer he spoke, the more I realized that I was experiencing a transformational revelation. I was living in denial. If I continued to make excuses, I would head down a road that could lead to serious life consequences. I would stay stuck, unhappy, and a discount version of myself. Something had to change, and it had to change now.

After delivering the bad news, my trainer told me something I would never forget. "But you know what?" he continued. "We are going to work on this together and get you better." It was the first time in my life that someone gave me such terrible news so bluntly, but was willing to help me take the steps I needed to turn things around.

That evening, I went home and began developing a plan with my wife. We cleaned out our kitchen and pantry, throwing away anything that was processed or high in sugar. We researched healthier restaurants nearby and ordered new cookbooks filled with healthy recipes.

If I was going to reverse my poor health, I knew I had to change my lifestyle. That meant being honest with myself about my priorities and restructuring my schedule to make room for proper self-care. Breaking old habits and forming new ones would be challenging, but the revelation that I needed to change my life was enough motivation to push forward. I spent the next year working closely with my doctor, exercising daily, and learning to eat healthier. By the end of my fitness journey, I felt like a new man. Not only did I lose over sixty pounds, but I also felt energized, happy and secure. Self-care became a fundamental element of my life. To this day, I continue working out and eating nutritious meals, and I have never felt happier and healthier.

The Feedback Loop of Life

The thing about life is that it is never static. Like being on an escalator, it is constantly moving. Whether you are standing still or walking forward, the one thing that life promises you is that in the future, you will arrive at a destination. The question is, where are you going? Are you on an escalator that is moving you upward or downward? Are you living a story with a happy ending or a tragic one? Have you chosen your destiny, or has life chosen it for you?

For years, I had been living my life like a man standing still on an escalator headed straight to the bottom of my physical health. Denying my obesity meant that despite my deteriorating health, I gave myself no reason to change. That lack of acknowledgment of my poor health meant I put little to no effort into taking care of myself. My lackluster efforts led to even worse results. I was stuck in a negative life feedback loop. My only way out was to break the cycle and rebuild my life from top to bottom!

Is there an area of your life where you feel stuck in a negative feedback loop? Do you repeat certain behaviors that make you feel weaker? Is there something you know is true but you have been denying, avoiding, or putting off?

Four Parts of a Negative Life Feedback Loop

As a life coach, I have found that when I delve deep enough into a client's problem, almost always there is a negative feedback loop present. A negative feedback loop is composed of four elements that work together to reinforce a set of detrimental outcomes.

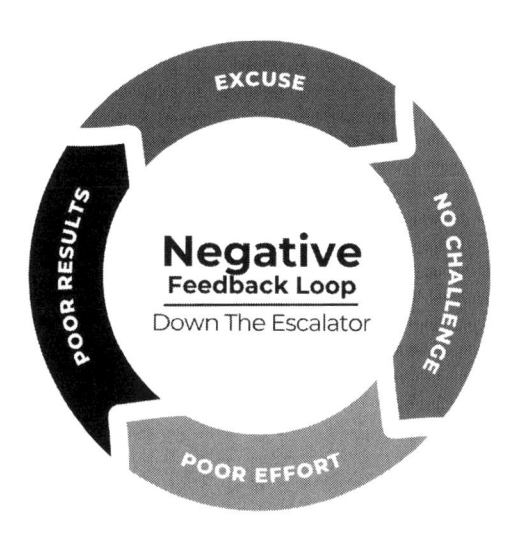

Negative Feedback Loop
Down The Escalator

- EXCUSE
- NO CHALLENGE
- POOR EFFORT
- POOR RESULTS

PART ONE | Excuse - If there is a problem in your life, it is likely that an excuse has been made somewhere. An excuse is a lie we tell ourselves about ourselves, to defend, protect, or justify our actions or inaction. Excuses hide the inner pain we feel or mask the shame we carry. It's like how I would ask my wife every Sunday how I looked before going on stage. I was looking for validation that everything was okay, but deep down I knew it was not. If you ever find yourself in need to believe something, it's time to stop and re-evaluate, even if it's incredibly painful.

Are there any statements that you tell yourself about yourself that you need to believe, but deep down you know are lies? Perhaps you are overweight, stuck in a bad relationship, or have a dead-end job. When you give yourself reasons why you can't fix your problems, you cement yourself in your setback.

PART TWO | No Challenge - When we make excuses for ourselves, we also remove the challenge that needs to be overcome. Like the man or woman who gets drunk every night but is "not an alcoholic" and "could stop any time," they always have a reason to keep drinking. When you don't have the courage to admit the truth, there is no reason to put yourself in the difficult, necessary position of taking responsibility, doing the hard work, and being victorious in the face of your challenges.

I am telling you right now that your life matters too much not to take responsibility. There are too many people waiting for you to become the person you can be. Today, decide you will always take on any challenge life presents to you.

PART THREE | Poor Effort - The saddest thing in the world is to see a good person with unlimited potential squander their future because of a lack of effort. When you don't have something to struggle against, a challenge to overcome, or a vision to aim for, you won't do the hard work that is required to break bad habits and start new ones.

PART FOUR | Poor Results - There is a powerful story in the Bible about two farmers. One farmer works his land and has abundance, while the other farmer chases fantasies and receives nothing during the harvest. The simple truth of life is that poor efforts will ultimately lead to poor results. We will not see the fruits of our labor or the gains from our hard work. We are destined to see the same mediocre results in the future as we have in the past.

Negative Life Feedback Loop Example 1
Ignoring my weight gain and its negative effects on my health meant I didn't take action, and my poor efforts resulted in me becoming sicker, heavier, and more depressed with no end in sight.

Negative Life Feedback Loop Example 2
Ignoring my personal finances meant I took no action to balance my household budget, and I slid deeper into crushing debt.

Your Success Feedback Loop
In the Bible, there is a concept called repentance. To repent means to change, to turn away from something, and to pivot direction. It is also an idea that is closely related to the practice of confession, a verbal recognition of one's past sins, failures, and shortfalls.

Repentance is a powerful practice that billions of Christians have practiced worldwide for more than two thousand years. To truly repent does not mean to say you're sorry and repeat past sinful actions again. It describes a true turning away from one's old life and embracing a new one. It is about starting again and letting God make new, exquisite wine out of old and broken wineskins.

The concept of repentance perfectly explains the experience of metamorphosis. In order to experience true life transformation, one must not only come to terms with their excuses, but also rebuild, retool, and ultimately re-order their life around their transformational moment of self-honesty. One must create a set of habits that will not keep them where they are but will take them to where they want to go. They must get off the escalator that is taking them down and get on the escalator that will take them all the way to the top!

Four Parts of the Success Feedback Loop

Throughout my career, I have been blessed with working with some genuinely successful people in life, family, and business. Almost always, the engine that pushes them forward is a well-oiled positive feedback loop. A positive feedback loop consists of four parts that work together to reinforce desirable life outcomes.

Success Feedback Loop — Up The Escalator
(ADMIT → CHALLENGE → MAXIMUM EFFORT → POSITIVE RESULTS)

PART ONE | Admit - When you have the courage to admit you have a problem, you've taken your first step toward overcoming it. To admit means to confess, acknowledge, reveal, or disclose. We admit when we come to the point where we can openly say what we know to be true.

PART TWO | Challenge - When we admit that something is wrong, we identify a problem that needs fixing. When we acknowledge something needs fixing, we begin the process of finding solutions and making changes.

PART THREE | Maximum Effort - When we identify a challenge, it will almost always inspire us to act decisively. That requires real effort to make the changes needed to see the improvements we want. That means putting the work into breaking bad habits and creating new ones.

PART FOUR | Positive Results - Maximum effort will ultimately lead to positive results. Over time, you will begin to see the fruits of your labor and the gains of hard work. That will mean better results, more opportunities, and a brighter future.

Success Life Feedback Loop Example 1 | Acknowledging my weight gain and its adverse effects on my health led me to finally take action, put in the hard work, and see meaningful life-changing results. With every lost pound, my willpower increased and I became more inspired to transform my life.

Success Life Feedback Loop Example 2 |
I acknowledged that my personal finances are in disarray. I finally took action, hired a financial planner, created a budget, and saw my savings increase.

The powerful thing about the Success Feedback Loop is that every pound lost, dollar of debt paid off, and base you hit, you will become more determined to build on your progress. Like the well-known "snowball method," small investments into yourself, over time, will grow into a gigantic avalanche of breakthroughs.

5 BIG LIFE FACTORS

Discovering the power of the success feedback loop can seem simple and even common sense. The sad truth is that most people do not dare to change what they know they should. They live their whole lives knowing *what* they need to do but never actually *do* it.

That is not you. You are not like other people. If you were, you would not be reading this book. You are the type of person who dares to break the cycle and is brave enough to rebuild themselves.

When it comes to creating your very own success feedback loop, here are five big life variables that will define long-term success and bring the greatest change.

LIFE FACTOR 1 | Mindset

Mindset is defined by the established set of attitudes, values, or core beliefs held by someone. It is the worldview that structures actions and the broader story that makes sense of new information. In simpler terms, how you choose to think about something will ultimately determine the outcome. Mindset is also a core variable, which is why it is number one on my list. What you believe will dictate almost everything else in your life.

Have you ever heard the phrase, "You are what you eat?" The same is true when it comes to mindset. You are what you believe. "We're finding the most graphic demonstrations to date of the power of the mind to affect the body," said Dr. Bennet Braun, a psychiatrist at Rush Presbyterian St. Luke's Medical Center in Chicago.[2] Dr. Braun and his team have shown through multiple studies how powerful the mind truly is. In one multiple-personality disorder study, they revealed that some patients experienced life-threatening food allergies for some personalities while other personalities experienced no measurable medical response. Translation, what you believe matters. Your mindset will set the tone for what will happen in the future.

LIFE FACTOR 2 | Romantic Partners

A Romantic Partner is your significant other or your spouse. As both a coach and a pastor, I have found that individuals with mismatched romantic partners have a hard road ahead of them. Their marriage typically ends in divorce, trauma, or pain, or they live a life of misery, destined to be with a person who has no interest in truly partnering with them to build a better life.

---

[2] Daniel Goleman, "Probing the Enigma of Multiple Personality," New York Times, June 28 1988, https://www.nytimes.com/1988/06/28/science/probing-the-enigma-of-multiple-personality.html

Finding the right partner is crucial for long-term success. That means finding someone who shares your values and long-term relationship goals. It also means finding someone you connect with body, soul, and spirit. A great partner will work with you to foster romance and create the conditions for amazing things to happen in your relationship.

LIFE FACTOR 3 | Social Relationships

Social Relationships are your friends and coworkers. There is an old saying that says, "Better be alone than surrounded by fools." As you become more successful, you will most likely go through seasons of loneliness. Why? Because loneliness is a byproduct of change. As you restructure your life and get serious about realizing your dreams, your social circles will change. That is why I live by the 30% rule:

- 30% of the time I spend with people who are higher achievers than me
- 30% with peers with similar goals and levels of success
- 30% with those I want to mentor and support
- 10% alone with myself. The most important relationship I have is my relationship with myself

LIFE FACTOR 4 | Environment

Environment is your surroundings. It's where you live, work, and spend time recreationally. As you update your mindset and make progress towards your goals, where you spend your time will change. Maybe you buy a house in a nice neighborhood, you go to an amazing church every Sunday, or you take vacations with your wife in the South of France. The environment you choose to spend time in will change the way you experience the world. Actively choosing environments that motivate you forward instead of holding you back will go a long way toward reaching long-term success.

LIFE FACTOR 5 | Mentors

I often tell my clients that the difference between having a mentor or not is the difference between spending one year accomplishing a goal vs. spending a hundred. In life, there is no better way to spend your time and hard-earned money than to seek out people who have been successful in the areas you desire to be successful in.

Psychologists have conducted numerous studies showing that human beings are designed to mimic the behavior of others. In a 1962 study, researchers at the University of Nebraska found that when two people sit down at a bar to socialize, they unknowingly mimic each other's similar behaviors such as posture, nodding their heads, rubbing their face, and touching their hair. [3] What is true in casual conversation is also true when it comes to success. The more you surround yourself with people you admire, the more you will take on their traits and behaviors knowingly and unknowingly. I regularly advise all my clients that they should strive to have a minimum of three mentors in the area of spirituality, finances, and career.

It's Time to Reset Your Loop

Success is the end result of mastering the art of creating positive feedback loops and breaking negative ones. Maybe you're obese, deep in financial debt, or stuck in a toxic relationship with no end in sight. Maybe you feel lost, hopeless, and powerless to habits that have broken you down into a discounted version of yourself. Despite the uniqueness of the crises you find yourself in, it's time to get serious.

Ask yourself these simple questions. If you had only one to two years left to live, would you continue to make yourself weaker, or would you have the courage to rise up and make yourself stronger? Would you leave this earth with a whimper? Or would you finally find your voice? Would your loved ones be unburdened by your passing or left better off because you lived?

If you can learn to harness the power of being honest with yourself

---

[3] Bandura A.1962Social learning through imitation. In *Nebraska symposium on motivation* (ed. Jones M. R.). Lincoln, NE: University of Nebraska Press

about where you are and where you want to be, you can experience a Metanoia that will change your life forever. You can finally break the cycle that's making you less than and practice behaviors that will make you more than. Now that you understand the anatomy, your next step is discovering the power of choice.

Positive Feedback Loop Cheat Sheet

It was productivity expert James Clear who said, "You do not rise to the level of your goals. You fall to the level of your systems." The most impactful change you can make in your life is to create a fine-tuned success feedback loop that will propel you to the life you want. Here are five simple steps you can take to maximize all five Big Life Factors along your journey!

STEP ONE | Renew Your Mindset

Every day, renew your mindset. Be willing to challenge your pre-existing beliefs and expose yourself to new ways of thinking and solving problems. Actively strive to be a student who is always learning, growing, and achieving new challenges.

STEP TWO | Invest In Your Romance

It's tempting to put your love life on the back burner. But don't do it. Invest in your romantic partner. Schedule time at least once a week to do something romantic. If you're single, set the conditions for meeting the right romantic partner who's headed in the same direction as you are.

STEP THREE | Foster Great Relationships

There is an old saying that states, "Birds of a feather flock together." Surround yourself with friends and business associates with character and integrity. And remember, live by the 30% rule.

STEP FOUR | Choose Your Environment

Choose to be in an environment that motivates you forward instead of discouraging you. For easy reference, spend time with people you admire, see how they live, and make a shift.

STEP FIVE | Find Great Mentors

Surround yourself with at least three mentors you admire in the areas of spirituality, finances, and career. Learn what they have to teach you and be willing to exchange your behaviors for the good behaviors they model.

CHAPTER 2
PRINCIPLES

Success Principle #1
Start with metanoia.

Success Principle #2
Admit you need help.

Success Principle #3
Break the negative feedback loop.

Success Principle #4
Start creating positive feedback loops.

Success Principle #5
Take control of the five "big" life factors.

Chapter 2 Exercise
EXAMPLE | YOUR IDEAL LIFE

The first step in building the life you want is to define your personal definition of success.

Describe your ideal life in 5 years.

I start my day early, waking up at 6 AM. Three days a week, I work out with a personal trainer at 6:30 AM and focus on light weightlifting. On alternate days, I engage in cardio for 45 minutes. My weight is at my desired level of 190 pounds, being 6 feet tall. I am in great physical and emotional health. My relationship with my romantic partner is thriving, as we make time for date nights once a week. Additionally, every Friday is dedicated to spending quality time with our children as a family. Financially, we are comfortable with our home being fully paid off and my business experiencing growth.

What are three steps you can take toward manifesting your ideal life this year?

1. *I am going to meet with my financial advisor to create a financial strategy for myself and my family.*

2. *I can hire a personal trainer.*

3. *I can plan an annual vacation with my spouse and kids.*

Chapter 2 Exercise
YOUR IDEAL LIFE

The first step in building the life you want is to define your personal definition of success.

Describe your ideal life in 5 years.

What are three steps you can take toward manifesting your ideal life this year?

CHAPTER THREE
Success Is a Choice...Literally

According to most research, statistics, and logic, a person who grew up under the circumstances I did should have ended up living a life of poverty, crime, and addiction. That was the story of many people raised in a similar environment as I was. Most of my early life was spent watching friends and neighbors suffer, struggle, and eventually make choices that too often led them down the wrong path. Even in my youth, I was determined to have a different fate. Something in me refused to settle for what life had given me. There had to be more, and I was going to find a way to reach it.

Right around fifteen years old, I received a revelation that would change my life forever. I realized that even though I was not the smartest kid, the most talented, and certainly not the most advantaged, there was still one powerful thing I could do that would dramatically increase my odds of success. If I could learn how to make the right choices, it wouldn't matter where my journey began. Instead, as long as I could conquer decision-making, I could get to where I wanted to be.

Realizing the power of my choices transformed my whole life from that point onward. It was like discovering a secret superpower that put me on the same footing as every other person on earth in the game of life.

Even though I could not choose the crisis I had found myself in, I could *decide* how I would respond—living with wisdom, victory, and peace. If I could make the right decisions today, I could create the future I wanted tomorrow.

The Hard Truth Is…

Most people don't even realize that they have the power to choose how to respond to their most significant challenges. Not having a strategy for making decisions almost always means responding to life instead of creating the desired life. To respond means to answer, encounter, reply, or retort. When we don't have a decision-making strategy, we are left to react in three potential ways:

1. **Emotionally** - This occurs when emotions are the decisive factor in your choices. Maybe someone hurt you, so you respond out of pain, lash out, and justify your actions. Maybe someone took advantage of you, so you seek revenge against them. Maybe someone made you feel small, so you respond with timidity. When you respond emotionally, you victimize yourself. You doom yourself to live a life responding to the world around you instead of being a force within your life.

2. **Past Experiences** - This occurs when your past is the decisive factor in your choices. Maybe someone broke your heart, so you think you will be heartbroken in future relationships. Maybe someone broke your trust, so you protect yourself by refusing to trust others. It's all too easy to let the pain of your past dictate your future. If you're not careful, you can miss new experiences and opportunities that can reset and redefine what is possible.

3. **Shallow Desire** -This is when people make decisions based on someone else's vision for their life. Maybe your parents wanted you to be a doctor, so you've spent your whole life working toward getting accepted into medical school. Maybe you saw someone on Instagram with a mansion, and now your dream is

to become rich. In a world dominated by celebrity culture and social status, it's easy to spend your whole life chasing desires and wants you don't need or really want. Thinking critically about what matters to you will save you from heading in the wrong direction.

Roger Martin, the dean of the Rotman School of Management, defines strategy as, *"An integrated set of choices that positions you on a playing field of your choice in a way that you win."*4 That means if you want to win the game of life, it begins and ends with effective decision-making. If you can make the right choices, you can take the right steps toward achieving your biggest goals and dreams. If you know how to respond to great challenges, you can meaningfully control the outcome.

Mastering the Art of Choice

In his book *How To Become A Straight-A Student,* bestselling author and productivity expert Cal Newport studied the real-life strategies of the highest achieving Ivy league students. What he found was astonishing and defied all expectations. Those at the top of their class not only got straight A's and perfect scores, but they were also heavily involved in campus life, extracurriculars, and collegiate sport. In fact, many, if not all, even studied fewer hours than their peers in the process. How were they able to do it? Newport explains that their success came down to making better choices. Where the average college student spent hours slaving away in the library semi-focusing, these select few kept daily schedules, practiced full-focus studying techniques, and streamlined their note-taking. In layman's terms, they got really good at making the right choices. The end result was superior academic success with more free time for campus life. What applies to Ivy League students also applies in life. Choices mean everything. Developing an excellent decision-making strategy is, quite literally, the difference between success and failure in every domain of life. If you can master the art of making choices, there is no limit to what you can do.

---

4   Roger Martin, A Plan Is Not a Strategy, Harvard Business Review, June 29 2022.

The Paradox of Sacrifice

When my wife and I decided to get married, we had just enough money to pay for a small, simple wedding. During our betrothal, we also felt God called us to start Awakening Church. The problem was we did not have enough money to have the wedding of our dreams and answer God's call to face our fears, take the leap of faith, and invest our own money into starting a church. After several weeks of intense prayer and seeking the Lord, my wife and I decided to downsize our wedding so that we could use the money to start our new church.

It was the biggest financial decision of our lives. Yet, we felt God was divinely leading us to do it. At that time, it felt like a huge sacrifice. After we made this sacrificial commitment, something miraculous happened. Within days of our private decision, people started calling and asking us what we needed. Friends and family bought us suits and dresses. Others paid for flowers and donated decorations. The restaurant we planned to have our reception at gave us an incredible deal and even allowed us to pay the bill after the wedding. In the end, we got our dream wedding for only 30% of what it should have cost us and we had the financing we needed to start Awakening Church. Today, Awakening Church is the fastest growing church in Bulgaria. My wife and I could not be happier as a married couple. Most, if not all, of the friends who helped us are still close to us to this day!

People often ask me, "Who gave you the seed funding for Awakening in the early days?" I reply, "We did!"

There is a lesson in this story and if you learn and apply it, it will transform the way you look at sacrificial giving. Amazing things happen when you are willing to sacrifice the present for a better future. That's the paradox of sacrifice. That is why it is the foundational principle of every wealth-building strategy in the world. To have more in the future, you must be willing to invest your current valuable assets. The more you are willing to give up now, the more you will receive later. It's that simple. If you *choose* to make decisions that will help you yield better long-term results, even at the cost of short-term satisfaction, you will unleash a level of wealth and blessing that will change not only your life but also the lives of your children's children.

Six Steps to Making Great Choices

Here are the six steps I use daily to make my most important decisions in life, family, and business. I hope you can use them to create your own decision-making strategy that will lead you to achieve the success you want.

STEP ONE | Refer To Principles

There is great value in your past experiences. If you are in a situation where you have to make an important decision, odds are you might have the expertise to help you make future decisions.

To quote hedge fund manager Ray Dalio, "You don't achieve happiness by getting rid of your problems. You achieve it by learning from them." The best advice you can give yourself is always found in your past experiences. When you make important decisions about your future, review the principles you have previously learned through past experiences that can help you in the present moment.

STEP TWO | Neutralize Yourself Emotionally

When you find yourself in a crisis, you are most likely emotionally invested in your situation's outcome. The more you are personally invested in the outcome, the more likely you are to make an emotional decision. I can tell you from experience that the worst decision you can make, regardless of your situation, is an emotional decision. Why? Because the more emotional a decision is, the less likely that decision is based on facts, reason, and logic.

The great billionaire investor, Charlie Munger, once said, "It is remarkable how much long-term advantage people like us have gotten by trying to be consistently not stupid, instead of trying to be very intelligent." This same investing principle applies to general decision-making. The key to making the right decision is to eliminate as many bad choices as possible. When you remove your emotions from a decision, you can make better decisions that will serve your long-term goals and interests.

STEP THREE | Assess Your Risk

Every choice you make comes with a certain set of risks and rewards. The key to making any good decision is to limit as much downside as possible while also increasing your upside. You can dramatically increase the quality of your decisions by thinking critically about potential outcomes before you make a decision:

1. **Assess Your Reward** - *Imagine what your life would be like if your choice worked out! What would the benefits of your decision be? How would your life change for the better?*
2. **Assess Your Risk** - *Imagine what your choice would result in if things didn't go your way. What would happen? How would your life be affected? Finally, could you live with your decision and the consequences of your choice? If the answer is yes, then the risk is worth the reward. If the answer is no, then the risk might not be worth it.*

It was Philosopher Cornel West who said, "There is a price to pay for speaking the truth. There is a bigger price for living a lie." In other words, the more honest you are with yourself about the risk and rewards of your choice, the more likely you are to make the right decision.

STEP FOUR | Assess Your Values

Several years ago, I got a call from a business executive who was going through a very challenging time. After hearing his story, he asked me if I could be his coach and mentor. The catch was that he could not afford to pay my regular fee even though he made a lot of money. Hearing the desperation in his voice, I decided to take him on as a client and coach him for free. If he wanted to pay me at some point, I told him to give the money to charity instead.

For months I worked with the man and helped him greatly. Over time, his situation began to improve. The problems he faced in his personal and professional life began to turn around. At some point, we stopped working together, and our paths moved on.

About six months later, I got a call from a dear friend who asked if the man I had coached was a client of mine. "Yes! We did work together," I told him. "How is he doing?"

"Not well, Maksim. He's been telling everyone around town that you demanded super high fees for coaching services and that you're only in it for the money!" When I heard those words, I was floored. I immediately felt a pain in my chest and the sting of heartbreak.

I had poured so much into this man. Honestly, I even considered him a friend. Throughout our months-long relationship, I never charged him a single cent to help him. Why? Because I did not become a coach to make money. I became a coach to help people. Despite my best efforts to sow into this person, he felt the need to lie about me all over town. I would be lying if I said it did not hurt my feelings. It was painful. But I could not let one man deter me from what I knew to be right—the call to help those who needed it.

It's easy to let moments of pain rob you of your purpose. That's why values are so important. The more value-driven you are, the more pain you can endure to do what you know is right. This is important because life is full of pain. You can either spend your time trying to avoid it or have the courage to live your values even when life is hard.

Before making a choice, ask yourself, "Will I like myself after? Will it give me peace? In five to ten years, will I be happy with my decision, and who I have become?" The more your choices align with your values and ultimate purpose in life, the more your decisions will lead you toward manifesting your true goals and desires. The more your choices take into account the needs and desires of your future self, the more you will set yourself up for success.

STEP FIVE | Assess What You Know (And Don't)

Several years ago, I had a friend who invested heavily in bitcoin. For months he would call me weekly and say, "Maksim, you have to buy bitcoin! It's the future." Despite my initial interest in digital currency, I would decline every time. Frustrated, my friend asked, "Maksim, why won't you invest?"

My answer was, "Bitcoin sounds promising. I'm sure it's worked out great for you! That said, I don't invest in things I don't know much about."

When you're making a potentially life-changing choice, do plenty of research. Some of the best decisions I have ever made came from educating myself. The more you are willing to educate yourself before making a decision, the more successful the decision will be. Therefore, take every opportunity to be a student of life. Be willing to admit what you don't know and confident enough to ask the "stupid questions" that only someone who knew nothing would ask.

STEP SIX | Seek Experienced Advice

I want to tell you a secret. 99% of what you want to accomplish someone somewhere has already failed and succeeded in. Before you make a big decision, put in the effort to seek out experienced advice.

The ultimate enemy of every good decision is ego. If you think you are smarter than everyone else and that you already have all the answers, you are destined to fail. If you don't have enough humility to ask questions and be a student of life, things will not go well. If you want to make the decisions that will bring success, be willing to ask questions, challenge what you think you know, and seek out the advice of those who have walked the path before you.

CHAPTER 3
PRINCIPLES

Success Principle #1
Refer back to lessons in the past.

Success Principle #2
Neutralize yourself emotionally.

Success Principle #3
Balance risk versus reward.

Success Principle #4
Align your decisions with your values.

Success Principle #5
Seek experienced advice.

Chapter 3 Exercise
EXAMPLE | RISK VERSUS REWARD

The key to making any good decision is to limit your downside as much as possible while also increasing your upside.

Choice: *Should I leave my job and start my own business?*

1. Assess Your Reward
Imagine how your life would be different if your decision produced the results you wanted. What would be the benefits of your decision?   *I've wanted to start my own business for years. It could give me the autonomy I've always wanted, the income I've always desired, and the opportunities I've been waiting for.*

2. Assess Your Risk
Imagine what your decision could mean if things don't go your way. How would your life be affected? Finally, could you live with your decision and the consequences of your choice? If the answer is yes, the risk is worth the reward. If the answer is no, the risk might not be worth it.   *I would lose my salary. That said, I have roughly saved up 1-year worth of overhead in my savings. Even though there is risk, I feel confident enough in my abilities and have enough savings to start my new business.*

Chapter 3 Exercise
RISK VERSUS REWARD

The key to making any good decision is to limit your downside as much as possible while also increasing your upside.

Choice: _____

---

1. Assess Your Reward

Imagine how your life would be different if your decision produced the results you wanted. What would be the benefits of your decision?

---

2. Assess Your Risk

Imagine what your decision could mean if things don't go your way. How would your life be affected? Finally, could you live with your decision and the consequences of your choice? If the answer is yes, the risk is worth the reward. If the answer is no, the risk might not be worth it.

PART TWO

It Starts With First Principles

There is a concept in physics called "reasoning from first principles." The idea is simple: take complicated problems, break them down into their most basic elements, and reassemble them from the bottom up. It's an easy strategy anyone can use to find answers to complex life questions. If you examine the problem of manifesting dreams and goals in each area of your life, your first step is to begin with the first principles of success.

Your first principles are the building blocks of true knowledge and wisdom—the right use of them. In life's journey, there are three fundamental principles that every other success principle is built upon, activated, and empowered by: the first principles of faith, action, and courage. If you can harness the power of faith, unleash your outer potential, and act with courage in the face of your greatest fears, I promise you that there will be no stopping you. It's time to step into the life that your destiny is calling you to manifest.

CHAPTER FOUR
The First Principle of Faith

Man is what he believes in.
Anton Pavlovich Chekhov

In the mid-twentieth century, famed Positive Psychologist Martin E.P. Seligman and his team wanted to explain why some people were successful in their pursuits and others were not. He concluded that it came down to how people responded to failure.

Some who experienced setbacks developed a behavior called "learned helplessness." Learned helplessness is an inner belief that an individual cannot change or control their life situation even when opportunities present themselves. To put it more directly, those who lost faith could not change their fortune. Even when their luck would change, their lack of faith meant they could not capitalize on new opportunities.

However, those who could "bounce back after a brief period of malaise"[5] did so because they continued to have faith. Despite their setbacks, they

---

[5] Martin E. P. Seligman, "Building Resilience." On Mental Toughness, (Harvard Business Review Press, 2018), pg 26.

did not give up and could experience real breakthroughs in their life. They continued to have faith despite their flaws and failures. "We discovered that people who don't give up have a habit of interpreting setbacks as temporary, local, and changeable."[6] In other words, people who kept their faith would find a way to get back up. People who lost faith would stay down, stuck, and in the same place they desperately desired to leave.

The lesson of Martin E.P. Seligman's reasoning is simple. Faith matters a lot. In fact, it's more often than not the difference between ultimate success and failure. When faced with a great challenge, crisis, or storm, your first step must always be to have faith and believe you can make it through. Even when things seem hopeless, you're feeling lost, or you can't see a way through, don't lose your faith. Nothing lasts forever. Even the worst storms pass, and the Sun will rise again.

What Is Faith

Faith is the belief in something that is unseen. It is having trust and confidence that a future that does not exist will happen. Living by faith means believing you can achieve your goals, even if the odds are against you. In that sense, faith is also not something just reserved for the religious, those who believe that God will work on their behalf. The truth is, all successful people I've met, coached, and worked with have all been people of great faith, regardless of their religious beliefs or practices. Why? They all had enough faith to take the risks required to achieve their success. They believed in themselves, their vision, and their dreams until the impossible became possible.

A number of years ago, I started playing golf regularly. The tranquil nature of the game, often played in a peaceful natural setting, offered me time to relax and get away from my busy schedule. Eventually, my family and I began taking trips to a beautiful mountain golf resort famous for its breathtaking views of the peaks and summits. This resort also had fantastic service, incredible amenities, and fine dining. On one particular trip, I spoke with the owner of one of Bulgaria's most prestigious golf resorts. This

---

[6] Seligman, page 27.

man had accomplished incredible feats in his career and personal life. But as I presented him with a leader-bound Bible, a book filled with stories of men and women who had achieved greatness through faith, he scoffed. "Pastor," he confidently declared, "I am an atheist. My entire family is atheist. We haven't had a Bible in our household for generations!"

His words stung, but I couldn't help but burst out in laughter. Startled, the man looked at his daughter and her fiance sitting across the table. "Do you believe in such fairytale things?" He asked his daughter's fiance. "I guess I don't! You see, pastor, it's not just my family. It's the whole region here that is atheistic. We do not believe in anything."

I laughed even harder.

"Why are you laughing?" the man asked insecurely.

I replied, "I find it particularly amusing that a man with as much vision as you, who has raised an incredible family, built a multi-million dollar business, and created a legacy of success for the whole city, doesn't see himself as a man of faith."

He looked at me, still not fully understanding where I was heading.

"How did you decide to build this golf resort?" I asked. He told me about the first time he came to the forest before the golf course was built. He imagined the whole layout such as where the five-star hotel would go and what he wanted his guests from all over the world to experience.

"Did anyone show you drawings or a picture of the buildings before you bought the land?" I asked.

"No," He said, "I could see it all in my head."

He sat there in deep thought, slowly realizing that he had been living by faith all along. The most valuable gift he possessed, the gift of harnessing the power of faith, was the very thing that made him a fortune.

The Faith To Be Courageous

I was fifteen years old when I was asked to conduct my first funeral service. While riding the school bus home after school, I received a call from a friendly woman I knew from church. In a solemn voice, she asked me tenderly, "Maksim, I need to ask you something?"

"Of course!" I replied, both concerned and curious.

"Can you be the minister at a funeral?"

"A Funeral?" I exclaimed loudly! "Did someone recently die?"

"Sadly, yes," She explained. "A local family has just lost their precious little child. They have only attended our church once. However, when they did, you spoke and touched their hearts. They told us passionately that the only minister they wanted to bury their beloved daughter was the sincere young man who ministered to their family."

I was shocked and also very surprised. Being only fifteen years old, I had only spoken a few times at my church's small youth gatherings. I had no idea how to lead a funeral!

I quickly told her I was willing to do it, but I had to check with my senior pastor first. Unable to reach him, I called my church's associate pastor. After hearing my story, he confidently told me encouragingly, "I think you can do it! Do you know what to say?"

"Yes! I think so!" I said back somewhat insecurely.

He advised me that if I was willing to have a little faith and believe in myself, I should take the opportunity as a developing young leader. As a sign of support, he was even willing to change his plans so he could come and stand next to me as I performed the service.

After I got home, I quickly ran to the small closet in my bedroom to look for something to wear. After rummaging around, I found an old hand-me-down blazer someone had given me as a gift for my birthday the year before. With urgency, I put on my blazer, black pants, and the only pair of formal shoes I had and headed to the local graveyard to perform my first funeral.

When I got there, it was raining heavily. The assistant pastor was already there with flowers for me to give to the family. As we walked in, I could hear loud weeping. Many who attended were incredibly emotional. There was a strong sense of injustice, tragedy, and shock that the life of someone so young was cut so short. Immediately, we were invited to speak to the sixty or so people in attendance. As I opened my Bible, the assistant pastor held a large umbrella above our heads to shield us from the rain.

The moment I opened my mouth, the atmosphere of the funeral completely changed. As I read from the Bible, attendees stopped weeping and started listening. Those who were passionately overcome with grief began to calm down and focus on my words.

I started by addressing suffering, how loss and even death touch every life at some point. I explained how sad it was when a life is cut short and that sometimes parents had to bury their children. In life, it is one of the most difficult types of loss.

Then, in a moment that I can only describe as divinely inspired faith, I asked the crowd, "How many of you would love to see this child alive again?" Everyone raised their hand. I continued, "He is alive on the other side of heaven with Jesus right now. Why? Because God takes the spirit of children who pass because they have an innocent soul."

"For those of us who are not so innocent, we have only one way to get to the other side and be with that child again. And His name is Jesus." Then I raised my hand and asked, "How many of you would like to receive Jesus into your life today?"

Every single hand in that graveyard was raised sky-high within a few moments. Then, I led the whole crowd in this simple prayer - "Dear Lord Jesus, I realize the shortness and value of life. I repent of my sin and invite you into my life to change me forever. Amen!

It was at that moment that I realized the true power of faith. Faith empowered me to step out of my comfort zone and do something I had never done before. Faith transformed this tragic moment into a catalyst for great change in the lives of everyone in attendance.

When you have faith, all things are possible. That's how the impossible becomes possible. When regular people believe that what is unseen can materialize and the future can be different from the past, they are inclined to act courageously. Why? Because faith is the foundation for all courage. If you can learn how to live your life by faith, there is no giant big enough who can scare you away from striving toward your dreams.

Harnessing The Power Of Faith

Both Psychologist Martin Seligman's insights into the power of faith and my experience as a fifteen-year-old boy are profound examples of the power of faith. They teach us one simple yet powerful truth. Achieving success without faith is like navigating a sailboat through an ocean without a sail. One does not exist without the other. If you have achieved success in any area of your life, it means that you have believed.

Faith is the key ingredient that, through vision and imagination, can take us out of our current limitations and into the world of the possible. When we learn how to harness the power of faith:

1. **Faith Can Encourage You** - According to the Oxford dictionary, to encourage means to give confidence and hope, to uplift, inspire, and motivate. When you are in the midst of great struggle, it is faith that will lift you up. It will inspire you to keep moving forward. It will motivate you to get back up and step

back out when you are knocked down. It will remind you who you really are and what you can do even when you fail.

2. **Faith Can Sustain You** - To sustain means to strengthen and support. It means to assist, help, and carry. When you are feeling the pain of short-term defeat, faith will keep you going, pressing, and believing. It will comfort you in tough times and assist you when alone. It will keep your dreams alive and carry you through crises of all kinds. When you have faith, you can weather any storm.

3. **Faith Can Open New Doors** - When you have faith, you can push back against the behaviors of learned helplessness. You will be able to see new opportunities, take advantage of breakthroughs, and keep your eye on the future instead of the past. When you have faith, what happened in your past doesn't have to define your future. Instead, it puts you in the right position for meaningful growth.

Faith In The Good

An underpinning value of western society that crystallized during the Enlightenment was the power of human progress. Progress is the belief that we can and should build a better, more open, inclusive, and prosperous world. This simple idea of having faith in what society could become and working towards it has radically shaped the modern world and changed the course of human history.

For over 100,000 years, human life expectancy was roughly twenty-nine years old. Life pre-civilization was terribly hard. Child mortality rates were incredibly high. The natural world was dangerous, untamed, and unforgiving.

The invention of cities, stable political institutions, and the post-industrial free market economy transformed the West and most of the world. In the past hundred years, life expectancy has more than doubled in the modern world. For the first time in human history, humans regularly live prosperous and enjoyable lives well into their seventies.

At the turn of the century, the average European and American lived on less than a dollar a day. Today, that number has exploded to unfathomable levels of wealth by historical standards.

All of this growth, abundance, and progress that has defined life in the modern world is the direct result of the millions of men and women who chose to live by faith and not by sight.

Every medical breakthrough, company, and technological marvel has been created by people who live by faith. Every marriage, loving parent, and financial investment is made by faith with the hope that the future can be better. The more we believe in the good, the more we will live by faith. The more we live by faith, the bigger our dreams become.

Faith In Others

As a coach, I often counsel people experiencing great suffering. They might have experienced a divorce, lost their job, or lost a loved one. In many cases, their pain has caused them to close up, lose trust, or isolate themselves. Regardless of their specific situation, I would always give the same advice. I would encourage them to never lose faith in other people.

For every soldier who destroys a building with a missile, someone else builds a house. For every crime committed, there is a gift of charity. For every act of manipulation, there is an act of nobility and virtue. Sometimes, it's easy to let our pain convince us that there is no light in a dark world. However, nothing can be further from the truth. Despite how bad things might get, there is always hope.

The great Mahatma Gandhi said, *"Where there is love, there is life."* The love we have as human beings for one another can turn any situation around. That's why having faith in others is so important. It's the invisible force that keeps the world turning.

Imagine a life where you did not believe in people. When you board a plane bound for Hawaii, you must believe that the pilots are who they say they are. When you feel sick and go to the doctor, you have to trust that your doctor went to medical school and knows what he is doing. When you go to the bank and make a cash deposit into a checking account, you have to believe that the bank teller won't take your deposit home with them at the end of the day. When we believe in other people, we open ourselves to opportunities that only teamwork, collaboration, and cooperation bring. If we continue to have faith in others, the future can always be brighter, and the final chapter has yet to be written.

Faith In God

A common argument against the existence of God goes something like this: there can be no God because there is too much evil in the world. As convincing as this argument might sound, an unavoidable logical fallacy is embedded within the argument—the binary nature of good and evil. If it's possible to choose to be good, they also have the choice to act nefariously. In order to have love in the world, there must be the danger of hate. To have peace and harmony, there must be the risk of conflict and chaos. Reality is a balancing act between chaos and order, left brain vs. right brain, and light vs. dark. For extreme evil to exist, there must also be the existence of an ultimate good.

To believe in God means having faith in the existence of a supreme good. To put it another way, God must exist, or at the very least, the belief in God must exist. It's that belief that structures the very framework of ethics and the world of value. Without a supreme good or a universal value hierarchy, there is nothing calling forth order from the chaos. There is nothing driving us to choose love over conflict and grace over retribution. To put it as Dostoevsky did in *The Brothers Karamazov*, "If God does not exist, then everything is permitted." If God does exist, then there is a way out of the dark.

This is the reason why faith is the first principle that speaks to the deepest parts of ourselves. It inspires us to see what could be in the face of what is. It empowers us to strive for justice in a world full of injustice. It inspires us to fear the Lord, love our neighbor, and seek the kingdom. Living by faith brings heaven on earth.

Faith In Yourself

Several years ago, my team and I decided to have a conference in the small mountain town of Samokov, Bulgaria. The event would be the climax of a national promotional tour for my first book, *Seven Decisions That Will Change Your Life Now*. The venue we chose was a four-thousand-seat arena close to the center of town. As we told the venue manager what we wanted to do, he shook his head and said, "There's no chance you'll be able to fill the arena. Even when we had the most popular singer in Bulgarian history perform, she couldn't even fill it up!"

As my team and I strategized how to fill such a large event space in a town of only thirty thousand residents, I had a moment of self-doubt. Sure, we had put on successful conferences before. However, when we did, we were in larger cities and had well-known speakers. In this case, it was just me who was speaking. Despite my initial fears, I knew I had to have faith in myself. In my heart, I believed that what we were doing was right. To reach the next level of success, I had to be willing to step up and step out in faith to make it happen. That's exactly what we did.

On the night of the conference, we were overwhelmed by the response. Not only did we fill every seat available, but over five hundred people stood outside, unable to get in. We even had reports of people fighting our ushers as they attempted to find a way past the gates. In the end, over ten percent of the whole city had come to hear me speak. To this day, it's one of the largest events our team has ever put on. It's also the largest audience that has ever come out to see me speak.

When we have faith in ourselves, we make decisions that build ourselves up. On the other hand, when we give into self-doubt, we often neglect self-care, speak negatively to ourselves, and make decisions that dehumanize and break us down.

The First Principle of Faith

Having self-confidence and the courage to bet on oneself and follow one's dreams is of the utmost importance. Those who struggle with self-worth, waver in their dreams, or feel overcome by fears and insecurities must understand that this road leads to nowhere.

Always be willing to move forward, get back up and try again, and never lose hope. If you can have the courage to believe in yourself and live by faith and not by sight, I assure you that your life will be transformed.

How To Build Faith In Yourself

Building faith in yourself is an important step towards achieving your ultimate desires. It requires both mental and emotional effort. The good news is, if you have the courage to believe in yourself, you will also discover that you are stronger, more powerful, and more capable than you ever thought possible! Whether you're feeling unsure about your abilities or facing a challenging situation, here are four simple but powerful steps you can use to build the confidence and self-assurance you will need to succeed in the face of your giants.

STEP ONE | Practice Positive Self-Talk

One of the most powerful ways to increase faith in yourself is to change the way you talk to yourself. Start by replacing negative thoughts with positive affirmations such as "I am capable and strong" or "I trust in my own judgment and abilities." Repeat these affirmations daily and write them down in your journal, diary, personal notebook, or daily planner. Take notice of the difference in your attitude and mindset when you purposefully speak positively over yourself.

STEP TWO | Set Realistic Goals

Having clear and achievable goals can help increase your faith in yourself by giving you a sense of purpose and direction. By setting goals that you can achieve, you set yourself up for success. With every goal you accomplish your personal faith and self-confidence will grow.

STEP THREE | Take Action

Sometimes, the best way to build faith in yourself is to start taking massive and immediate action toward your dreams. Even small steps can turn into an avalanche of momentum and increase your confidence along the way. It's much easier to overcome challenges when you see yourself making meaningful progress.

STEP FOUR | Surround Yourself With People Of Faith

The people you surround yourself with can significantly impact your mindset. Surround yourself with positive and supportive individuals who believe in you and love you enough to keep you accountable to the person you are becoming.

CHAPTER 4
PRINCIPLES

Success Principle #1
Don't forget - faith is the foundation of courage.

Success Principle #2
Believe in the good.

Success Principle #3
Believe in others.

Success Principle #4
Believe in God.

Success Principle #5
Believe in yourself.

Chapter 4 Exercise
EXAMPLE | HARNESS THE POWER OF FAITH

The key to harnessing the power of faith is to learn how to believe.

---

1. What Are You Believing For (Daily Challenge)
Write down what specific things you are believing for today?

Today I am believing for breakthroughs in my business and for favor in every area of my life. I believe that I will not only meet clients, but that I will also meet the right clients. I believe for provision for my family—for health and wealth for myself, my wife, and my kids.

---

2. What Are You Believing For (Monthly Challenge)
Write down what specific things you are believing for this month?

This month I am believing that I will find a great mentor who can guide me as a leader and business professional. I believe that my daughter will get accepted by their dream college and that my son will make the honor roll at school!

Chapter 4 Exercise
HARNESS
THE POWER OF FAITH

The key to harnessing the power of faith is to learn how to believe.

1. What Are You Believing For (Daily Challenge)
Write down what specific things you are believing for today?

2. What Are You Believing For (Monthly Challenge)
Write down what specific things you are believing for this month?

CHAPTER FIVE
The First Principle of Action

"I am not what happened to me.
I am what I choose to become."
Carl Jung

When I was a child, I loved spending time outdoors. For several years, we lived next to a local forest. Every day I would spend hours looking for berries, tracking small animals, and exploring it with other neighborhood kids.

I also had a tendency to get regular scrapes and bruises. More often than not, I would come home with splinters and thorns, typically under my fingernails.

Without fail, my grandma would greet me at the door and check for scuffs and scratches I might have gotten while in the forest. She was a fantastic woman who was also exceptionally smart and kind. As my caretaker, she would look out for me, and help me. She was a role model and a source of unlimited love and support.

One day, while I was in the woods, a huge thorn got lodged under my fingernail. Once it penetrated my finger, I felt a sharp and piercing pain. Within seconds I began to imagine what my grandmother would have to do to get it out. She often used a nail cutter to cut deeply before she used tweezers to pluck out the remainder of the thorn.

Wanting to avoid the pain of past experiences, I attempted to pull the thorn out myself. With every attempt to reach it, I pushed it in further. Eventually, the thorn was so deep I could not even touch it.

When I got home, I placed my throbbing hand behind my back as I walked by my grandma. Noticing my hand was conspicuously placed behind my back, my grandma asked, "Why are you hiding your hand?"

"I'm not hiding anything. I promise!" I lied in a desperate attempt to convince her nothing was wrong.

"Come here and show me your hand! I know you're hiding something."

Once she saw the thorn and how deep it was lodged under my fingernail, her demeanor quickly changed. She now understood why I had hidden it from her and sensed the fear and discomfort in my voice.

"Oh, my child!" She said gently, "Why are you always doing this to yourself?"

While holding me close, she told me something I would never forget. It was a truth that would be imprinted in my mind forever and save me years of future suffering, struggle, frustration, and pain. "Maksim, if we don't fix your hand and remove the thorn now, you might avoid pain. Over time it will fester and get infected. But, if you can be brave enough to take action now, it will hurt only temporarily. Once it is removed, the healing process can begin."

My grandma's wisdom taught me a valuable lesson I have lived by every day since. When we find ourselves suffering, we can take immediate action to change our situation. It might be painful initially, but it will lead to an incredible transformation in the long run. Maybe you find yourself in a toxic relationship. Maybe you want to leave your current job and start a new business, or maybe you have to face a personal fear you've been avoiding. In every situation, the choice is clear. Avoiding a wound will only lead to infection and disease. An untreated infection can leave lasting damage or even become fatal. Alternatively, if you are willing to act decisively in the face of fear, you will always be able to change the direction of your situation.

Overcoming Fear

In his New York Times bestselling book *Extreme Ownership: How U.S. Navy Seals Lead And Win*, Navy Seal Commander Jocko Willink explains how to take decisive action regardless of the battlefield. He writes that it's easy for leaders to let fear get the best of them. When they do, fear will always lead to inaction. *"It is critical for leaders to act decisively amid uncertainty; to make the best decision they can based on only the immediate information available."*[7] In a warzone, being unable to make decisions and act decisively could be the difference between life and death for you and your platoon.

The same principle that applies to combat also applies to life in general. We all have to make important decisions concerning life, family, and business and know full well that personal bias, blind spots, and lack of information might affect our choices. We can make very few decisions knowing 100% of the data. Accepting action as a first principle to success means acknowledging that inaction is never a good strategy. You must become comfortable with chaos and uncertainty and get good at making the best decision confidently.

It's Time To Take Action

Put simply, action is the step or process of doing something to achieve a desired goal or aim. It's having the courage to put enough energy,

---

[7] Jocko Willink, Leif Babin, *Extreme Ownership: How U.S. Navy Seals Lead And Win* (St. Martin's Press, 2017) pg. 254.

movement, and force into bringing meaningful change to a given situation.

In layman's terms, it's making it happen regardless of the roadblocks and obstacles in the way. Knowing how to take immediate action is a powerful tool and it can transform your life. If your goal is to improve your relationship with your romantic partner, it's not enough to acknowledge that your relationship needs work. It's decisive action that gets you across the finish line.

Several years ago, a coaching client called me for counsel. He said, "Maksim! I suffer greatly in my marriage. I want to have a relationship like you have with your wife. I want to find happiness!"

I said, "Great, what's the first thing you do when you wake up in the morning to serve your wife? Do you tell her you love her, maybe cook her breakfast? Do you ask her how she slept or what she needs help with today?" The man was in dead silence on the phone. It had never occurred to him that to have a happy marriage, he had to be willing to take meaningful action toward his desired goal. He had been unhappy for years and never considered what *he* could do differently to turn things around.

I explained to the man that the happiness my wife and I experience daily was on purpose. Theodora and I have a wonderful relationship because we both choose to act every day to achieve that happiness goal. We choose to communicate, serve each other, and be accountable to one another. I explained to the man that having a happy romantic relationship takes more than just saying "I do" on your wedding day. It takes both partners making daily decisions that move them toward the goal of a more perfect union.

The moment we are willing to take meaningful, decisive action towards the lives we want, regardless of the fear we might feel, is when the future we want becomes genuinely possible.

Fix What You Know Is Broken

In his bestselling book, *The One Thing: The Surprisingly Simple Truth about Extraordinary Results,* Real Estate Mogul Gary Keller tells the story of how, for years, he found himself in a cycle of poor results, professional failure, and personal frustration. His big breakthrough came when he was finally brave enough to ask himself one simple question that would change his life forever. *"Finally, out of desperation, I went as small as I could possibly go and asked: "What's the ONE thing you can do this week such that by doing it, everything else would be easier or unnecessary?"*[8] At that moment, Keller learned a universal lesson that had the power to transform his whole life and explode his business. When you choose to fix what is broken, amazing things happen.

If you are willing to be honest with yourself, you know you have "one thing" you should fix. Maybe you're overweight and think about how different your life would be if you weren't. Maybe you have unpaid debt that hovers over you like a dark cloud. Maybe there's an issue with an employee, and you haven't mustered the courage to have the tough conversation. Whatever your "one thing" is, I want to tell you right now that you need to address it, confront it, and fix it. You need to be courageous enough to act decisively in the face of fear, chaos, and uncertainty. The more willing you are to fix what you know is broken in the present, the more you can expect to receive in the future.

Get Good at Taking Action

It was the great Canadian Psychologist Jordan Peterson who said, *"If you fulfill your obligation every day, you don't need to worry about the future."* Put differently, when you can take meaningful *regular* action in the short term, you will always be able to reach your goals in the long term.

The difference between average people and successful people is *regular* action. One of the main reasons why most people never achieve their

---

[8] Gary Keller, Jay Papasan, The One Thing: The Surprisingly Simple Truth Behind Extraordinary Results (Rellek Publishing Partners, 2013) pg. 4.

goals is that they give up too quickly. They take massive action to fix what they know is broken, only to quit after not seeing immediate results. Most diets fail not because the diet wasn't effective but because the person on the diet couldn't stay consistent. In other words, they stopped repeating what was working.

Another reason why people fail is that their actions are not significant enough. They make minor changes effectively. However, progress is never truly made because the gains are not significant enough to build upon. That's why setting goals that are ambitious and achievable is so essential.

Thomas Edison once said, "Our greatest weakness lies in that we give up easily. The surest way to succeed is always to try again." Translation, your worst enemy is not your biggest giant or your scariest foe; it's the inner you who has given up on your dreams and goals.

Win in Every Season
While doing my regular review of the real estate market in the region, I found something that caught my eye in one of my favorite neighborhoods of Sofia. The location was incredible, and the view was stunning. It was surrounded by open space inadequate for new developments. Then suddenly, Covid-19-19 hit the country and drastically changed the housing market.

One afternoon, I went online to check how construction was going. I saw that the price of my favorite house had dropped significantly. It was clear the owners were unsure if they could sell it in this new economic environment. For a moment I hesitated. Thinking about buying a home during a global pandemic seemed risky on the surface. However, after running the initial numbers, I knew this home could be a once in a lifetime opportunity. Despite my reservations, I decided to take immediate action and reached out to the owner.

Upon further inspection, I learned why the price had dropped. First, the builder of the home had been accused of fraud. The owner of the house had paid him upfront to build the home. Before it was finished, he had spent all the money. That caused a lawsuit between the owner and builder that led to a settlement. Second, the corner of the yard was over a water pipeline. That meant if the pipeline was ever in need of repair, the cost of fixing it would be cumbersome. In a post-Covid-19 economic environment, these two complications had made the home unattractive to most potential homebuyers. For my family, however, it could be perfect.

As quickly as possible, I got on a call with the property owner. In our negotiation, I brought up Covid-19, the construction problems, and the water pipeline. I expressed to them my interest in making a quick deal. I offered them cash. If they were willing to sell me the unfinished house for half the listing price, I could write them a check tomorrow! My family and I would own an unfinished house that we could make into our dream home with more investment. They would finally be rid of a house that had plagued them through construction issues and a lawsuit. With little hesitation, they said yes!

The end result was truly extraordinary. During the first year of Covid-19, my wife and I invested hundreds of thousands of dollars into the property to convert it into our dream house. After construction was complete, we got the home re-appraised. It was now worth three times what we paid to both purchase and renovate the home. That's the power of knowing how to take action. The best opportunities rarely reveal themselves at the ideal time. If you have the courage to act in the midst of a crisis, you can master the art of creating value in every season.

Keep Moving Forward

There is hardly anyone who hasn't heard about President Abraham Lincoln. He is widely considered to be one of the most remarkable figures in world history and the most significant president in US History. However, did you also know that he grew up poor? His mother died when he was only nine years old. He struggled his whole life to overcome incredibly tough personal, political, and professional failures.

A Timeline of Abraham Lincoln's Life:

- 1809 - Abraham Lincoln was born.
- 1816 - Due to his family being forced from their home, he began working at seven years of age.
- 1818 - His mother died when he was only nine years old. However, his entrepreneurial spirit propelled him to work even harder to support his remaining family.
- 1831 - Abraham experienced his first business failure and was left penniless.
- 1832 - He ran for political office and lost. In the same year, he lost his job and failed to get into law school.
- 1833 - He borrowed money from a friend to start his second business. Quickly, his second business failed and left him with debt that took him seventeen years to pay off.
- 1834 - He ran for local public office again. This time, however, he won his first race for the Illinois House of Representatives.
- 1835 - Abraham proposed to Ann Mayes Rutledge, his first love. Tragically, however, she died several months later. He was left devastated.
- 1836 - Abraham experienced a nervous breakdown. He spent six months in bed. His failing health left him on the brink of life and death.
- 1838 - Fully recovered, Abraham decided to run for speaker of the house. While winning re-election as an Illinois House Member, he lost the election.
- 1840 - He wins a fourth term in the Illinois House of Representatives.
- 1843 - Ran for U.S. Senate and lost.
- 1846 - Won an election to become a U.S. congressman. He would demonstrate an excellent aptitude for national politics.
- 1849 - His term expired, and he did not win re-election.
- 1849 - Lincoln attempted to be named commissioner of public lands and failed.
- 1854 - Ran for U.S. Senate and lost again.
- 1858 - Ran for U.S. Senate again. He won the popular vote but lost the election to Douglas.
- 1860 - Lincoln won the election as the first Republican president of the United States. Over the next five years, he became one of, if not the most, consequential presidents in American history. He ended slavery through the Emancipation Proclamation and led the Union to win the American Civil War.

It's easy to assume that great individuals were always great. In reality, nothing could be further from the truth. In the case of Abraham Lincoln, despite his many failures, challenges, and obstacles, he never gave up. In the end, what made him great was his persistence. Lincoln never gave up despite immense difficulty in his life.

That's what you have to do. Despite your faults and failures, never give up. That means keep climbing to the top, regardless of how steep the path might be. Make the decision every day to move forward. I promise you, if you do, you will reach your mountaintop.

How To Take Action

It's not always easy to take meaningful action when you feel stuck, frozen, or powerless. Here are three simple yet effective steps you can take to break through fear and act towards your purpose.

STEP ONE | Choose a Clear Target

In order to pull the trigger decisively, you need a target. A target is needed for accuracy. Identify a specific goal you hope your decision will achieve.

Most people go wrong when making decisions because they confuse identifying options with selecting targets. Research has shown that when we have too many options, we struggle to identify what we want. In a 2000 study, Columbia University Psychologists Sheena Iyengar and Mark Lepper showed that too much choice leads to inaction. When shoppers were provided with twenty-four types of jams in a large display at a local supermarket, interest increased, but sales went down. On another day, shoppers were only given six choices in a small display. What happened? Sales immediately went 30% up.[9] This simple lesson has profound implications. We are more likely to take action when we identify potential choices and define exactly what we want to accomplish.

---

[9] Sheena S. Iyengar, Mark R. Lepper, When Choice is Demotivating: Can One Desire Too Much of a Good Thing? Washington University, 2000. https://faculty.washington.edu/jdb/345/345%20Articles/Iyengar%20%26%20Lepper%20(2000).pdf

STEP TWO | Stop Doubting Yourself

To re-quote Navy Seal Master Trainer Jocko Willink from earlier, *"It is critical for leaders to act decisively amid uncertainty; to make the best decision they can be based on only the immediate information available."* Don't overthink the decision-making process.

When I was in high school, I was called into my teacher's office after a big test. Showing me my exam, he pointed out how many questions I had gotten wrong. He also pointed to my eraser marks that showed I had initially chosen the right answers before second-guessing myself. When you're taking a life test, don't re-check your answers more than once. Go with your gut. Your first choice is often the correct one.

STEP THREE | Don't Deviate from Plan "A"

As an executive coach, I hate hearing the words "Plan B" from a client. Why? Because when most people say "Plan B," they mean a different goal entirely. Instead of becoming a doctor, Plan B is to become a veterinarian. Plan A might be to start a business. Plan B is to get a regular job. That is not a change in plan. It's a change in goals and outcomes.

I teach my clients that there is a difference between having a Plan B and a contingency plan. Where a Plan B is a change in target, a contingency plan is a change in strategy to reach your target. In life, don't create Plan B. Instead, have contingency plans. Get good at regularly making adjustments to your plan while staying the course toward your goals.

CHAPTER 5
PRINCIPLES

Success Principle #1
Act decisively to change your situation.

Success Principle #2
Fix what you know is broken.

Success Principle #3
Get good at taking regular action.

Success Principle #4
Create value in every season.

Success Principle #5
Keep moving forward.

Chapter 5 Exercise
EXAMPLE | YOUR ONE THING

It's time to fix what you know is broken.

What Is Your One Thing: *My messy house*

---

1. Describe your life if your 'One Thing' was fixed?
What would your life be like? How would things be different?

I would come home to a clean, ordered home, and peaceful household. When I wake up in the morning I can get ready in my organized bathroom. I could cook meals in my kitchen without having to do the dishes beforehand. They are already done. I can spend quality time with my spouse and children in a functional living space. I can work from home in a clean home office that isn't covered by papers.

Choose three adjectives you would use to describe how you would feel if your one thing was fixed: *Calm, Peaceful, Focused.*

---

2. What are three actions you can take in the next thirty days to fix your one thing?

---

1. I can clean my house from top to bottom.

2. I can make a list of organizational supplies I need and buy them online.

3. I can hire a cleaning service to clean my house once a month.

Chapter 5 Exercise
YOUR ONE THING

It's time to fix what you know is broken.

What Is Your One Thing: _____

---

1. Describe your life if your 'One Thing' was fixed?
What would your life be like? How would things be different?

Choose three adjectives you would use to describe how you would feel if your one thing was fixed: _____,_____,_____

---

2. What are three actions you can take in the next thirty days to fix your one thing?

1.

2.

3.

CHAPTER SIX
First Principle of Courage

*"Vulnerability is not about winning or losing.
It's having the courage to show up even
when you can't control the outcome."*
Brené Brown

As a child, I was consumed by fear. The fear of being left abandoned and rejected. My first experience with this fear was at a kindergarten boarding school. On my first day, I was shocked when my mother told me she would only come to visit once a week. Every night, I would sit on the top of the stairs facing the front door with tears streaming down my face as I waited for her to return. Despite her reassurance, the fear of abandonment lingered. It followed me throughout my childhood. Even as a teenager, I still struggled with it. I couldn't sleep in the dark and had a nightlight by my bed every night. But one day, everything changed. I was at church on a Wednesday night, and during the offering my pastor shared the story from the Gospel of Matthew where Jesus teaches his disciples how to handle fear. He said, "Do not worry about tomorrow, for tomorrow will take care of itself. Each day has enough trouble of its own." At that moment I realized that my relationship with God had become a powerful force in my life. It gave me the courage to face my fears head-on and overcome them. From that day on, I was no longer a prisoner of my fear. I became a warrior ready to conquer any challenge that came my way. I had heard this story many times before, but that day was different. I was ready to listen to the wisdom of Jesus in a new way.

As I stood there, torn between my fear and the voice within me, a wave of emotions washed over me. I was consumed by the memories of the abuse my mother experienced and my constant struggle for survival. I thought of all the times I had gone to bed hungry and all the nights I had cried myself to sleep. I had lived with fear and insecurity all my life. At thirteen, I had moved dozens of times. The story was always the same. My mother's abusive relationship meant we regularly bounced around from house to house. My mother and her boyfriend would get into a fight. He would beat her loudly and sometimes even publicly. A neighbor or landlord would witness the beating and then ask us to leave.

My constant hunger made me feel extremely insecure. Not eating for a day or two was a regular occurrence. When I could get money, I would stretch what I had as far as I could.

That day at church, I was lucky enough to have two Bulgarian Lev, worth roughly one American Dollar, in my pocket. I had already planned to use that money to buy breakfast at school for the next two days.

While the minister led the church in the offering, something deep within me said, "Maksim, give your two Lev away."

"What?" I asked myself. The small bill was the only money I had. Just the thought alone gave me instant fear and anxiety. "What would I eat then tomorrow or the day after?"

But then, something shifted. I realized at that moment, I had a choice. I could continue to be controlled by my fears and insecurity, or I could step out in faith and trust that something greater than myself would provide for me.

When the offering basket came around to me, I did the unthinkable. I put the two Lev into the basket. As I let go of that money, I felt a sense of release and freedom. It was as if a weight had been lifted off my shoulders. I realized that in that moment, I had taken the first step towards overcoming my fears and living a life of courage.

From that day forward, I started to see my life in a new light. I learned to trust in God's provision and to step out in faith, even when it was difficult. I learned that courage is not about being fearless, but about facing our fears head-on and choosing to act despite them. Through it all, I found that by giving away what I thought I couldn't afford to lose, I was able to gain something far greater: a life of freedom and purpose.

Despite the insecurity and uncertainty that plagued my life, I found the courage to rise above it all and make a difference in the world. I realized that I had the power to be my own person, make my own choices, and let courage define my decisions. In that moment, all fear and anxiety that had consumed me for so long suddenly vanished, and I knew that everything would be alright.

With a renewed sense of hope and determination, I walked out of the sanctuary. What happened next was truly miraculous. A complete stranger approached me. With a look of certainty in her eyes she said, "I feel that God spoke to me and asked me to give you this." Then, she handed me a bill worth ten times more than I had just donated. My jaw dropped.

This was the first time in my life that I genuinely felt like I could be courageous enough to step up and make a difference in the world.

From that moment on, my mentality shifted. Despite the ongoing struggles with poverty and insecurity, I began to give to the church every week, believing that if I did my part, God would send resources my way. I realized that my life would be radically different if I dared to face my fears, choose to be an overcomer instead of a victim, and be a contributor instead of a taker. If I continued to face my fears and walk in courage, there was no limit to what I could achieve.

The Problem of Fear

There is a reason ancient religious texts of all kinds call Satan the Father of Lies. Why? Every lie he speaks is based on fear. Every person experiences fear. Maybe you are struggling with an illness and fearful that you might not get better. You are in debt and are scared that there is no way out. Maybe you're suffering from anxiety, depression, or PTSD and are scared you'll never feel like yourself again. It doesn't matter. Even though each of us has our own unique set of challenges and worries, at the center of each of them is fear. If you're not careful, you can let your fear keep you down when life is calling you to rise up.

What Is Fear?

Fear is an unpleasant emotion caused by the belief that someone or something is dangerous. It means terror, fright, alarm, panic, or agitation. Fear is a universal experience that every human being and mammal alike encounters. There are two kinds of fear that we experience:

TYPE ONE | Fear of the Past - Pain from past experiences can create fear in the present. Maybe you were cheated on in a relationship, so now you experience the fear of infidelity in future relationships. Maybe a dog bit you when you were a kid, and now you experience a fear of dogs. Your past experiences of pain or suffering have led you to perceive similar future experiences as potentially painful. Fear caused by past experiences can be particularly insidious and hard to overcome. Why? Because there is already a baseline for pain. The only way forward is to have the courage to re-expose yourself to potential pain points and work through what might come your way.

TYPE TWO | Fear of the Unknown - One of the most powerful evolutionary advantages humans have over other animals is the ability to imagine the future. We can project what we think might happen and make decisions today that prepare us for tomorrow. Our ability to think about time linearly provides us with the ability to think critically, strategize, and express ourselves artistically. The downside of imagination is that we can also imagine negative consequences and outcomes that might not be there. Put simply, we can feel fear just by simply being unaware of the future. If we're not careful, we can let ourselves be gripped by fear.

Regardless if you're experiencing fear caused by the past or of the unknown, all fear can be traced back to the ultimate fear we have as humans of death. Maybe you are afraid of snakes because you don't want to be bitten. The underlying fear behind the fear of being bitten is the fear of death as a result of the bite. Kids often wake up at night and are gripped by fear of monsters under their beds. This is an adolescent imaginary response to wrestling with the reality of mortality.

Fear is not necessarily a negative thing in itself because it is a natural instinct we developed as species for survival. If you were in the African Savannah and you saw movement in the bush, your fight-flight response could be the trigger that saves you from being eaten by a lion. The problem arises when we find ourselves stuck here. We could end up believing that behind every rock is a lion waiting to strike. Fear can grip us and keep us from progressing.

The Fear Perspective

A few years ago, I was coaching a sales executive who was in charge of managing hundreds of associates. During a large group session, I asked her in front of many of her co-workers, "What is your biggest fear?" The moment the question left my lips, I could see the immediate discomfort on her face.

With trepidation, she began to explain, "I am very good at selling one-on-one. I built my entire career on knowing how to sell. However, when it comes to public speaking in front of my whole team or a bigger crowd of people, I freeze up and become afraid!"

After she finished, I asked her to describe in detail how she physically felt when she had to speak in front of an audience. "I feel my hands get sweaty and shaky. I feel my heart beating faster, and my mouth gets dry. I become hyper-aware of my surroundings." she said.

I quickly changed the topic on purpose and asked her a different question, "Tell me about what excites you and gets you going?"

Looking a bit confused, she answered, "I really get excited when I get to travel. In fact, just recently, I traveled to Rome with my fiance. It was amazing!"

"How did you feel physically when you hopped off the train in Rome for the first time?" I asked.

She replied, "I felt so excited! My heart was racing. I felt hyper-aware of my surroundings, and my hands got sweaty. I was giddy with excitement." As she finished her description, people from all over the room began to pick up what I was getting at. She was describing feelings of excitement in the same way she described her experience of fear. The only difference was one was seen from a positive perspective, and the other was seen from a negative one.

"Do you get what I'm doing?" I asked.

The moment of realization hit her like a bolt of lightning. In that instant, she understood the profound truth I had been trying to impart. The difference between excitement and fear was nothing more than a shift in perspective.

We all face fear in our lives, but how we choose to see it ultimately defines us. A gazelle may flee from a lion, but once the danger has passed, it goes back to grazing. For humans, fear can linger and consume us, leaving us trapped in a state of constant flight.

But what if we could choose to see our fears as opportunities? What if we embrace them and harness the power of courage to overcome the challenges that once held us back? Like a hunter who becomes the predator, we too can shift our perspective and rise to greatness.

The Solution of Courage

Clinical Psychologist and best-selling author of *Twelve Rules For Life* Jordan Peterson often publicly recounts when one of the students asked him, "What do you do if something is chasing you?" To put it another way, what do you do when confronted with great fear, anxiety, or even doubt?

Peterson answered, "Turn around!" The only way to overcome the things that are chasing us is to have enough courage to face them.

When fear grips you, it's easy to let it consume you and cut you off from your potential future. I know this all too well. When I first felt called to ministry, I struggled with fear about where my life would end up. I saw the ministers around me. They seemed poor, overweight, uneducated, overworked, and unhappy. Their wives also seemed tired, overworked and burdened by the challenges of life. I thought that saying yes to ministry meant I would end up just like them. My fear almost blocked me from my destiny.

But I didn't let it. I refused to let fear control me. I began to look outside my own network for inspiration on what ministry could be like. I found it. I found new models of success that I could follow. Eventually, I worked up the courage to say yes to my calling and start Awakening Church.

The lesson here is simple: fear blocks you from your destiny, but courage is the antidote to fear. It's the medicine for the human condition. It's the force that leads you to your true purpose. Don't let fear control you. Have the courage to pursue your calling, no matter how daunting it may seem.

What Is Courage?

It's the ability to do something that frightens you or strength in the face of pain. It means to be brave and strive to be the hero of your own story. In this sense, courage is the opposite of fear. It is also a first principle of success because every great act begins with courage. A hero doesn't have courage because they are the hero. They are the hero because they have courage.

Does having courage mean you will never experience fear? No, quite the opposite. It means you are able to stop fear from controlling your actions. When something is chasing you, you don't have to respond by running away. Instead, you can face your dragon, fight the good fight, and ultimately become victorious in the face of danger.

Courage will often manifest in one of the Four C's of courage:

Crisis - Crises come in all shapes and sizes, from accidents and deaths, through pandemics and breakups, to divorce. In these moments, we can find ourselves facing great difficulty, pressure, and even danger. It's easy to feel overwhelmed and powerless in a crisis, but it's important to remember that we all have the strength to change our fortunes.

Conflict - When we find ourselves in great conflict, we often feel powerless to fight back. The story of the three hundred Spartan warriors who valiantly defended their homeland from the massive invading Persian army at the battle of Thermopylae, gave the world a shining example of what it means to stand tall in the face of adversity.

For a period of over three days, three hundred Spartan warriors were able to hold off an army of hundreds of thousands, preventing them from destroying the city of Sparta. This proves that the most powerful force on the battlefield is not the size of the army, but the courage and determination of individual people. This serves as an important reminder that even in the darkest of times, we all have the ability to rise above our circumstances and emerge victorious.

Consistency - I often say, "Consistency is the closest thing to a human superpower." The road to success is rarely a straight path. The American comedian Kevin Hart knows this all too well. When podcast superstar Joe Rogan asked about the path of his comedy career, Hart quipped, "Joe, I am a ten-year overnight success!" It's easy to look at successful people and assume that they got there by luck or chance, but the reality is that it takes an immense amount of consistency, hard work, and dedication to break through.

Comeback - One of the greatest lessons I've learned on the road to success is that a comeback is not a go-back. We often think of a comeback as trying to reclaim what we've lost or retracing our steps to what we missed. But in reality, a comeback is about so much more than that. It's about having the courage to get back up after we've been knocked down. So, don't be afraid to get back in the fight because the comeback is where the real magic happens.

When in Doubt, Believe in Yourself

A few years ago, I got a call from one of Bulgaria's well-known journalists and a television host named Martin Karbovski. He explained that a friend of his had recently attended Awakening Church and had told him about everything our congregation was doing. He was interested in doing a story about our work and invited me to be a guest on his weekly Bulgarian Prime-Time news show. At first, my wife and I were very weary of his request. In his reporting, Martin Karbovski had a reputation for being tough and often negative towards religious institutions. He had even been sued recently for unsubstantiated allegations he had made against organized religion. A negative story about our church could as easily have done irreparable harm. At the same time, his prime-time news show would also be seen by the majority of the country.

When I first told my wife that Martin Karbovski had called me, I told her, "No way I am doing this interview!" The fear that he might unfairly scrutinize me, my family, and my church was real. However, my attitude began to shift as we spoke more about it.

I thought to myself, "Maybe this could be different. It might also be a positive story! Maybe this wasn't a problem but an opportunity to share what God had called us to do with millions of people!"

That night, we decided to take the risk and say yes to the interview. However, we would have one condition. We requested that one of our own cameras could be present. In the event that the story was edited in an unethical way, we could release the interview in its entirety. Karboski's team agreed!

Initially, the interview was planned to only take twenty-five minutes. It ended up going over one hour. After we were done, we had no idea which questions or answers would make it on air and received no feedback on how they thought the interview went. My team and I had mixed feelings. We felt both fearful and optimistic. At the same time, I knew we had made the right decision. In life, you can't control every variable. That said, you can control it if you put your best foot forward. I knew in my heart that was exactly what we had done.

The night of the show, my wife and I eagerly watched from my smartphone. Karbowski began his show with a clip from Martin Luther King Junior's famous "I Have A Dream" speech. He went on to explain that there were few people in Bulgaria he could count on to speak the truth. After investigating myself and our church, He compared us to MLK. He believed everyone in Bulgaria needed to hear what I had to say and see the work we were doing.

After watching the one-hour special, I was completely floored. Karbowski had chosen our church and me to be one of the most positive stories he had done in his career. He had also given us the biggest open door we had ever received as ministers—to reach the entire country of Bulgaria in one night.

I learned a valuable lesson that night. When in doubt, bet on yourself. Don't allow fear to take away your voice or rob you of the opportunities life will present to you. When you find yourself at a crossroads, it's easy to doubt which path to choose. However, behind every challenge is the potential to find purpose. Behind every crisis is an opportunity to act courageously. When you are feeling the sting of self-doubt, don't give in. Believe in yourself and make the decision to take action. If you do, you will discover how capable you are and move the boundary of what is possible.

The Courage Of Helping Others

About nine months after I took a brave step forward and made my first act of giving to my church, I found myself experiencing a new level of freedom, agency, and empowerment. From that fateful night at church, I embraced every opportunity to give, serve, and lead. In doing so, I experienced a profound transformation of my mindset and perspective on myself, my value, and my boundless potential for the future. This was the moment when I woke up to the power of selfless giving. I understood that true personal empowerment began with the courageous act of putting yourself out there.

One morning, when I was about fifteen years old, I received a call from someone who worked for a foundation associated with our church. A large semi-truck full of toys, shoes, and clothes had just arrived, and they needed help unloading and distributing supplies to local people in need. My friend, who also lived in the ghetto, decided to go with me. Shortly after, we arrived to help unload the truck. We assumed that we would have additional help to unload this massive truck, but we quickly realized we were wrong. For the next eight hours, we unloaded every box.

As we completed our task, the foundation's supervisor thanked us for our efforts and offered us a reward. He allowed us to each pick an item from the truck to take home. My friend and I looked at each other and without hesitation both replied, "We can't take anything. These toys and clothes are for the needy." The supervisor was taken aback and asked if we both lived in the neighborhood. We replied, "Yes sir, we do, but there are others who need it much more than us."

This moment was a turning point for me, as it was the moment I realized how much I had changed in nine months. Though I lived in a house with no running water or electricity, I no longer saw myself as poor. Despite my lack of material wealth, I felt free, empowered, and able to be a problem solver. I wanted to be a help to others. I realized that true wealth and success does not come from what we have but from how we see ourselves and our impact on others. It was a moment I will never forget. It was the moment I understood the true meaning of selflessness and the power of giving.

True courage is not just about being a strong individual. It's about rising above our own fears and insecurities to act on behalf of others. It's about standing up for others, even when we don't feel like standing up for ourselves. When we are willing to serve something bigger than ourselves, that's the moment when we truly transform from being our own hero to becoming a hero for others. We become a beacon of hope, a light in the darkness for our children, family, and friends.

It's not always easy to step out of our comfort zone and put the needs of others before our own. But when we do, we tap into a wellspring of courage and strength that we never knew we had. We discover that we have the power to make a positive impact on the world and in the lives of those around us. Don't be afraid to step up and act on behalf of others. That's the true mark of courage.

It's Time To Increase Your Courage

I can tell you from experience courageous people are not born. They are made. Why? Fear is a universal experience. Every single person who has ever lived has wrestled with feelings of self-doubt, fear, panic, anxiousness, or distress. The difference between people and courageous people is that, despite how they feel, courageous people have learned how to push through and still do what they know they should do. Here are four steps that you can take to break through your fear, increase your courage, and achieve the success that awaits you on the other side:

STEP 1 - ACKNOWLEDGE YOUR FEAR

The first step to increasing your courage in a crisis is to acknowledge and accept your fear. It is natural to feel afraid in the face of uncertainty and change. It only grows stronger when we resist our fear and try to push it away. By acknowledging and accepting your fear, you are taking power away from it and giving yourself the space to move forward.

STEP 2 - REFRAME YOUR THOUGHTS

Your thoughts have a powerful influence on how you feel and how you respond to a crisis. When you dwell on negative thoughts or painful outcomes, try reframing them in a more positive light. For example, instead of thinking, "I can't handle this," try thinking, "I am strong and capable, and I will find a way through this." As you have learned in previous chapters, what you believe matters. Therefore, believe that you are stronger than you think and watch your inner self rise powerfully.

STEP 3 - TAKE ACTION

The third step is to take action. Courage is not the absence of fear but the ability to act despite it. When you find yourself paralyzed by fear, take one small step toward your goal. This can be as simple as getting out of bed, making a phone call, or even showing up to work. By taking action, you are proving to yourself that you are capable and that you can handle the situation.

STEP 4 - PARTNER WITH THE RIGHT PEOPLE

Finally, seek support from people who will build you up and speak life and faith into you. We all need help and guidance during difficult times. Don't be afraid to reach out to a friend, pastor, or mentor. Surround yourself with people who will lift you up and remind you of your strength.

It is important to remember that courage does not mean being without fear, but rather the ability to take action despite fear. By acknowledging your fear, reframing your thoughts, taking action, and partnering with the right people, you can increase your courage and navigate through the crisis with wisdom and resilience.

CHAPTER 6
PRINCIPLES

Success Principle Number #1
Face your fears.

Success Principle Number #2
Turn your fear into motivation.

Success Principle Number #3
Be the hero of your story.

Success Principle Number #4
When in doubt, bet on yourself.

Success Principle Number #5
Stand up for others.

Chapter 6 Exercise
EXAMPLE | DISCOVER YOUR COURAGE
Take inventory of your past victories.

---

1. Can you recall a moment when you experienced fear but ultimately summoned the courage to overcome it?
How did it change your situation and affect your life?

A few years ago my father passed away. My siblings asked me to perform the eulogy at his funeral. I don't often speak in public and I am generally intimidated to stand on stage in front of people. However, I mustered up the courage, wrote a eulogy speech, and shared about how amazing my father was.

My ability to overcome my fears led to beauty in the midst of such great tragedy.

---

2. Who are three people that inspire you to be courageous? What did they do that you admire?

---

1. My mother. She was a single mom who did an amazing job raising me.

---

2. My mentor. He built a large business from nothing. I admire him so much.

---

3. I admire Michael Phelps. He worked very hard to become the best swimmer in the world. I want to work as hard as him.

Chapter 6 Exercise
DISCOVER YOUR COURAGE

Take inventory of your past victories.

---

1. Can you recall a moment when you experienced fear but ultimately summoned the courage to overcome it?
How did it change your situation and affect your life?

---

2. Who are three people that inspire you to be courageous? What did they do that you admire?

1.

2.

3.

PART THREE

Discovering Your Inner Power

As the dawn of the industrial revolution broke, the steam engine emerged as the driving force behind the modern world. The high-pressure engine generated the power to fuel rapid technological innovation and economic growth and propelled society forward at an unprecedented rate. It pushed boats across the water and trains across continents. It revolutionized agriculture, paving the way for the automobile.

Like the steam engine that powered the modern world, I needed an inner power source. I needed to harness the power of pressure, identity, and habits to drive me forward, empower my abilities, and maximize my potential.

As I furthered my own journey of personal and professional growth, I began to see that pressure, when channeled correctly, could be a powerful motivator. I learned to use the pressure from a crisis to push myself to new heights. I also discovered the importance of understanding my own identity and purpose to shape my decisions. Finally, I learned how to use good habits in helping me stay on track towards achieving my goals. Through my own experiences, I realized that tapping into the source of your inner strength is the key to manifesting your outer purpose. With the right mindset and tools, you can harness the power of pressure, identity, and habits to achieve anything you set your mind to.

CHAPTER SEVEN
The Power of Pressure

"The idea of lying on a beach as my main thing just sounds like the worst—it sounds horrible to me. I would go bonkers. I would have to be on serious drugs. I'd be super-duper bored. I like high intensity."
Elon Musk

On July 6, 2001, an eight-year-old boy named Jesse from Mississippi was swimming with his family off the coast of Laguna Beach, Florida. He was on vacation with his family. Jesse loved the ocean. His favorite vacation activity was diving in the shallows just a few yards away from the shoreline.

Without warning, the unthinkable happened. The young boy abruptly disappeared from the surface of the water. Moments later, a terrifying scream was heard. As the thrashing waves turned blood red, nearby beachgoers froze as they realized a shark was attacking Jesse.

As Jesse's family panicked, his uncle quickly jumped into the water, wrestled the shark, and pulled the boy back to shore. By the time Jesse was out of the water, he was unconscious and in critical condition. The shark had bit his right arm off and a large part of his thigh. As local lifeguards and paramedics attempted to save Jesse's life, his uncle headed back towards the water. Calm and composed, he dove back and grabbed the shark. As everyone watched in amazement, the man dragged the six-foot predator onto the sandy beach. A few minutes later, an armed ranger approached and shot the shark three times in the head, killing it on the spot.

Due to the quick action of Jesse's uncle, the boy lived. The immediate medical attention Jesse received on the beach and in the hospital was enough to save his life. The uncle's decision to wrestle the shark to shore also meant Jesse's surgeons recovered the boy's arm, which was still in the shark's throat. After an eleven-hour operation, the surgeons reattached not only the arm but also the tendons and nerves. Eventually, the boy had full function of his bitten limb.

Within hours this incredible story of the brave actions of Jesse's uncle became a national story. Local media later asked the man what was going through his head during the shark attack. He explained that when he heard the screams of his nephew, he did not think twice. He was not gripped by fear. Instead, he knew he had to act swiftly. The reporter also asked him why he chose to jump back in the water to wrestle the shark. Jesse's uncle explained that his decision to go back into the water was intentional. He knew the shark was still in the shallows and had to be captured and killed before hurting someone else. He also knew if the shark swam away with Jesse's arm, his nephew would be disabled for life. "I couldn't allow that," the brave man said with conviction.

It's amazing how bravely people can act while under incredible pressure. History is full of stories of great men and women who, under extraordinary circumstances, rose up and acted courageously. In each case, what they did in relation to the pressure they experienced made them great.

There is a direct connection between pressure and potential greatness. Why? You need tremendous pressure to manifest incredible potential.

The more pressure you allow yourself to experience, the more you will unlock who you could be. That is the secret to greatness. Pressure is your greatest source of personal power that can drive you toward your desired achievement.

The Power of Pressure

I remember the first time I discovered the power of pressure. It was a warm summer afternoon, and my mother and I were hosting her dear friend and her young daughter at our house. We were playing with the older children on the street when suddenly I noticed the little girl had wandered onto the road.

At that moment, time seemed to slow down. As I watched in horror, our neighbor quickly backed his pickup truck out of the driveway, unaware of the danger looming ahead. My heart raced as I frantically shouted at the man, but my voice was drowned out by the engine's roar. The little girl, lost in her own world, looked down at a pebble, completely unaware of the danger. I was sure she would be crushed beneath the truck, and my heart felt like it would burst out of my chest.

But then, like a scene straight out of an action movie, the girl's mother sprang into action. With lightning speed and incredible courage, she jumped out from the yard, grabbed her daughter, and safely rolled under the pickup. The whole affair unfolded in the blink of an eye, but it felt like an eternity.

When it was all over, both the mother and daughter were miraculously unharmed. I was in awe of the mother's quick thinking and bravery. As I reflected on that experience as an adult, I realized that what saved the child's life was a combination of natural instinct and quick reasoning. The young girl's mother responded to the outer pressure in a way that unlocked her inner potential and saved her daughter's life.

As I witnessed the incredible bravery of that young mother, I couldn't help but wonder if there was a way to harness the power of pressure in my own life. I realized that instead of allowing pressure to paralyze me, I could use it to unlock my own inner potential and achieve incredible results. From that moment on, I made a conscious effort to view pressure as an opportunity to grow, learn, and push myself. I began to see that it was possible to spring into action and overcome challenges instead of freezing in the face of crisis. This realization transformed how I approached challenging situations, and I want to share the same insight with others, so they can harness the power of pressure in their lives and achieve their goals.

From Pressure To Power

When I find myself in a high-pressure situation, I take three simple steps to convert that pressure into power. First, I identify the source of my pressure. This means taking a step back and analyzing the specific events, situations, or people that are causing me stress. Understanding the root of my pressure helps me to know how to deal with it.

Next, I reframe my mindset about pressure. Instead of seeing it as a negative force that is holding me back, I see it as an opportunity for growth and development. Pressure can be turned into motivation that can push you to reach your full potential.

Finally, I take action. I know that simply recognizing the source of my pressure and reframing my mindset wasn't enough. Like the woman who saved her daughter's life, you must take specific steps to address and overcome the pressure. This can include developing healthy coping mechanisms, setting goals, and seeking advice from a mentor. By taking control of the situation, you can harness the power of pressure and use it to achieve your goals.

Unlocking Your Potential

I believe that everyone has the potential to be great. It's just a matter of unlocking it. It doesn't always take a shark attack or a life-threatening situation to do so.

Potential is the capacity to become something in the future. It's when something or someone is possible, likely, latent, developing, dormant, unrealized, and undeveloped. It's important to remember that we all have potential within us. It's just a matter of recognizing it and unlocking it.

Pressure is a continuous physical force exerted on or against an object. It can also mean influence, compulsion, provocation, persuasion, duress, or demand. Like heat, pressure can take the raw material of carbon and turn it into a diamond. Pressure can be uncomfortable and challenging, but it is necessary to help us grow and reach our full potential.

The more you seek comfort, the more you put your potential to sleep. However, the more you are willing to put yourself in situations where you face pressure, the more your potential begins to unlock.

Becoming Antifragile

One day, I made the bold decision to make my ongoing weight loss journey public. I told my family, friends, coworkers, and even my entire church community about my goals. I wanted to hold myself accountable, and I knew that the added pressure of others knowing my plans would push me to succeed.

For months, I worked tirelessly to achieve my goals. I stuck to a strict diet and exercise regimen, and I tracked my progress every step of the way. I knew that people were watching and waiting for me to fail, but that only motivated me to push harder. Every Sunday, I would see familiar faces in church, and they would ask me about my progress. Some would comment on the visible change in my overall appearance, while others would offer words of encouragement.

One Sunday, a lady approached me and asked why I had made such a big deal out of my weight loss journey. I thought about it for a moment and realized that the pressure of others knowing my goals had been a healthy one. It kept me accountable and pushed me to work harder. In the end, it paid off. I transformed my body, and I felt better than I ever had before. A little healthy pressure went a long way in helping me achieve my goals.

Healthy pressure also makes you *more than* resilient. In his bestselling book *The Coddling of the American Mind: How Good intentions and Bad Ideas are Setting up a Generation for Failure*, New York University Professor Jonathan Haidt explains why there has been an incredible increase in the anxiety and depression of young people in recent years. In 2012, only 6% of women suffered from a diagnosable psychological disorder. That number has almost tripled to 15% in 10 years and continues to grow.[10] Haidt and his team attribute this rise in psychological fragility to recent changes in safety-oriented parental values and new overprotective parenting norms.

He explains this psychological phenomenon with a concept called *antifragility* with a simple yet profound analogy about children. Adults don't let children play with a wine glass because a wine glass is fragile. That's why we give kids plastic cups instead. Plastic cups are very resilient. You can drop them, and they won't break. However, there is a third category called antifragile. Something that is antifragile is not only resilient (won't break under pressure), it gets better when it's stress tested. Haidt argues that the important psychological concept for adolescent development is that kids and adults are antifragile. Like the immune system that gets stronger through exposure to new viruses, kids get psychologically stronger when they undergo manageable levels of regular pressure. Overprotective parenting norms are, therefore, hurting young people.

The lesson - pressure won't just make you resilient, it will make you *more* than resilient. It will make you *antifragile*—a stronger and more capable version of yourself.

---

[10] Greg Lukianoff, Jonathan Haidt, *American Mind: How Good intentions and Bad Ideas are Setting up a Generation for Failure* (Penguin Books, 2019) pg 148.

Creating Healthy Pressures

As a child, I learned to thrive under pressure. Growing up in a home without electricity meant I had to adapt to taking cold showers. At first, it was a struggle, but over time I learned to love the feeling of the cold water on my skin. To this day, I still take cold showers every morning as a way to shock my body into action and prepare myself for the challenges of the day.

It wasn't until I was older that I truly understood the power of purposeful pressure. One day, I skipped my cold shower and noticed that throughout the day, my willpower for other challenging tasks was weaker. The next day, when I returned to my daily routine, I felt a renewed sense of determination and willpower. This realization hit me like a ton of bricks. The healthy pressure I applied to myself through my morning ritual directly impacted my ability to handle the pressures of life.

I learned that by mastering the art of outer pressure, I could unlock my inner potential. Whether it's a cold shower, a challenging workout, or time in the sauna, finding your own version of healthy pressure and embracing it can help you handle the pressures of life with grace and determination.

Maximize What Is Hard

What would happen if you treated every hard task, every tough challenge, and every difficult conversation as an opportunity to grow, stretch, and expand? What if you gave 100% of your effort in all that you did? What if you strived, fought, and contended with every day as if your life and the lives of those you loved depended on a good outcome? How much different would your day, month or year be?

What if you pushed yourself to maximize the resources you have and the opportunities you have been given?

The thing about life is the more you put into it, the more you get out of it. It's a lesson that has shaped my whole life. It's also why I created the Daily Success Journal. This ten-step system is designed to help you maximize every part of your day and, ultimately, every part of your life. The more willing you are to maximize what is hard, the more you will benefit from the fruit of your labor.

Don't Wait. Act Instead.

Whenever I approach the topic of procrastination, whether it's to my team at our offices, hundreds on a Sunday morning at church, or thousands at a conference, people respond in one of two ways. The first way is a silent but visible personal confession that they often fall victim to their procrastination habits. The second is also a quiet but visible longing to beat this invisible enemy that often robs us of our time and potential.

Here was my battle with procrastination. I remember myself on my own, living in a house with no water or electricity at fifteen years of age. I never wanted to go to school or get out of bed. Then again, what kind of freak would want to get out of a broken bed early in the morning during a cold winter with no heat?! Looking back, I laugh about it.

Today, my life looks very different than it did all those years ago. I still wrestle with procrastination every day. Yes, there are battles I'd prefer not to have, emails I'd rather not answer, or difficult conversations I don't want to have. Like the way I preferred the comfort and warmth of my bed as a teenager, I still prefer the comfort of staying at home with my family over the demands of a growing business.

I'd like to say I have won the war over procrastination every time, but I haven't. I have days where I win and days where I succumb to the temptations of enjoying the present. However, as in any war, losing one or two battles doesn't matter. Ultimately, victory comes by winning the war.

For me, the victory over procrastination happens by making three life-altering decisions:

DECISION ONE | TAKE RESPONSIBILITY - If you want to be successful, it's high time to understand and accept that the only person who can make your dreams happen for you is yourself. A person could have resources, knowledge, opportunities, and even the whole world. However, if they never take responsibility for their destiny, they will not succeed. The more responsibility you take for your life and your dreams, the more successful you will be in reaching them.

DECISION TWO | FOCUS ON WHAT'S MEANINGFUL - The most powerful weapon you have against this enemy is a higher purpose. Visualizing your future self living in your ideal life is often enough to give you the energy and power to push through the immediate feeling of hesitation.

If you wake up one morning and are stuck in the thralls of procrastination, ask yourself, "How would I act if I were the person I desire to become? What would they do at this moment? How would my day, week, month, year, and life be different if I rose up and won the battle today?"

DECISION THREE | ACT BEFORE YOU DOUBT YOURSELF - Do not delay. Don't voluntarily give in to your self-doubt and personal fears. Instead, accept that you deserve the opportunity to manifest what you know is in you. Feed that inner voice calling you forward by taking action even if it's just a small step. Every time you see yourself succeed, your confidence will grow. As your confidence grows, your inner drive and outer passion will ignite. Like a supercharged engine, your daily actions and incremental accomplishments will fuel you to aim higher, strive harder, and be greater in every area of your life.

It's extremely sad how many people live their whole lives captured by the enemy of procrastination. Their pressure has created a vacuum chamber starving their ideas, dreams, and desires of oxygen. They are like hamsters spinning on the wheel of life, stuck in one place and without energy to generate meaningful action. The more they procrastinate, the more they remain stuck.

Then, there are those who are simply surviving. They behave as if they are on the road to where they want to go, but, in reality, they live day to day only to postpone their desires and dreams indefinitely. Every new year, the resolutions are the same. They are always waiting for the right time, and there is always a reason why progress is not made.

Never allow yourself to fall into the trap of procrastination. Instead, use your daily pressure to become your inner power. Instead of letting your challenges break you, use them to make you. Be brave enough to fight for your future self by defeating procrastination in the present.

>Don't postpone what you are avoiding.
>Don't put off having tough conversations.
>Don't put off fixing what you know should be fixed.
>Don't put off vacations you want to take.
>Don't put off dinner with a friend.
>Don't put off calling your parents.
>Don't put off hugging your child.
>Don't put off saying I love you.
>Don't put off asking for forgiveness.
>Don't stop yourself from living.

Instead, take on the adventure of your life and live it to the fullest. Focus deeply and intently on who you know you can become and make the daily decisions you know you should make. If you do, you will undoubtedly accomplish your dreams.

CHAPTER 7
PRINCIPLES

Success Principle #1
Let pressure unlock your potential.

Success Principle #2
Maximize what is hard.

Success Principle #3
Take responsibility for your life and dreams.

Success Principle #4
Find your higher purpose.

Success Principle #5
Act before you doubt yourself.

Chapter 7 Exercise
EXAMPLE | DAILY SUCCESS JOURNAL

STEP ONE | Write down the time, place, and date.

| Time | *7:30 AM* | Place | *My Kitchen* | Date | *Monday* |

STEP TWO | Reflect on how you feel.

How do I feel from 1 to 5?					
1	2	3	**4**	5
Bad	It's Not My Day	So-So	**Happy**	Superb

STEP THREE | Explain the reason for your mood.

The reason I feel this way?
I just got a promotion at my work last week! Feeling excited about my new position!

STEP FOUR | Focus on what you have, not what you're missing.

Today I am grateful for:
I am grateful for my amazing wife and kids! I am grateful for my incredible career!

STEP FIVE | Meditate on what you desire.

Meditation and Prayer
Today, I desire to make a positive impact on those around me. To be a leader who empowers, equips, and supports my team at work and at home.

STEP SIX | Devote your time to what moves you forward.

What can I do now to feel better?

I can read my morning devotional. I think I need a little extra time with God today.

STEP SEVEN | Set your daily goals.

My most important goal for today is:

Share my vision for my team at work about what needs to happen over the next few weeks.

STEP EIGHT | Act with wisdom, passion, and purpose.

I will act exactly for this purpose because:

I want to be successful in my career in order to provide financial security for my family.

STEP NINE | Take one step closer to your ideal you.

One specific action that brings me closer to my goal is:

Review my quarterly to-do list and write my team an email outlining our strategic key objectives.

STEP TEN | Set a deadline for your work day.

Today I will stop working at:
5 PM

Chapter 7 Exercise
DAILY SUCCESS JOURNAL

STEP ONE | Write down the time, place, and date.

Time	*7:30 AM*	Place	*My Kitchen*	Date	*Monday*

STEP TWO | Reflect on how you feel.

How do I feel from 1 to 5?				
1	2	3	4	5
Bad	It's Not My Day	So-So	Happy	Superb

STEP THREE | Explain the reason for your mood.

The reason I feel this way?

STEP FOUR | Focus on what you don't have, what you're missing.

Today I am grateful for:

STEP FIVE | Meditate on what you desire.

Meditation and Prayer

STEP SIX | Devote your time to what moves you forward.

What can I do now to feel better?

STEP SEVEN | Set your daily goals.

My most important goal for today is:

STEP EIGHT | Act with wisdom, passion, and purpose.

I will act exactly for this purpose because:

STEP NINE | Take one step closer to your ideal you.

One specific action that brings me closer to my goal is:

STEP TEN | Set a deadline for your work day.

Today I will stop working at:

CHAPTER EIGHT
The Power Of Identity

*"I am not what happened to me,
I am what I choose to become."*
Carl Jung

In her best-selling book *The Gifts Of Imperfection: Let Go of Who You Think You're Supposed to Be and Embrace Who You Are,* Psychologist Brené Brown talks about the power of shame and how it often holds us back from reaching our full potential. She writes, *"Shame is the most powerful master emotion; it's the fear that we're not good enough."* Put another way, what we believe about ourselves structures what we do and who we end up being.

With every step we take, we are faced with two choices: believe we are unworthy or believe that we are worthy of greatness. It is a choice that can make or break us. Growing up without a father, I struggled for years with feeling I was worth less than my peers. I wrestled with self-doubt and the lie that I did not deserve love and happiness.

Over time, I learned how to let go of that belief. My faith taught me that

I was infinitely valuable in God's eyes. Discovering that empowered me to embrace my true self and believe I was worthy of all the good things life had to offer.

That's when everything changed. Knowing who I was unlocked my inner potential, and I started to see the world differently. I realized that worthiness isn't something that's earned or given—it's something that we already possess. When you choose to believe in yourself, you open the door to a world of possibilities. I urge you. Don't let your belief in your own unworthiness hold you back. Believe that you are enough. Watch as the real you courageously rises up.

It Starts With Identity

It was Mark Twain who said, "The easiest thing in the world is to quit smoking. I've done it a thousand times!" When it comes to changing your life, it's easy to start with attempting to modify your behaviors. If we desire to lose weight, we get a gym membership. If we want to change our financial situation, we create a budget. As Mark Twain points out, the problem with this strategy is that our behaviors are grounded in our beliefs and values. When we attempt to change our behaviors without changing what we believe about ourselves, we might be able to change for a little while, but over time we fail to experience true transformation.

Identity is...

Who or what somebody or something is. It's your name, specification, identification, and classification.

It's not by accident that the first thing God did after creating humans was giving the first human a name—*Adam*. In the Hebrew tradition, naming something gave it function, form, and purpose. Therefore, when God named the first human Adam, God did not simply give him a name. He gave him form, function, and purpose. In other words , God gave Adam an identity. That identity became the source of his potential, responsibility, and purpose.

This story from Genesis shows that every person has an identity. Whether someone consciously knows it or not, everyone has a set of beliefs they hold about themselves, what they are capable of, what their value is, and what they should become. All identities are made up of three interconnected components:

Your Beliefs - Beliefs are what you are convinced to be true based on both evidence as well as anecdotal experience. Our beliefs are our opinions, observations, faith, and reasons that we use to make sense of the world around us. Our beliefs have a profound influence on our own sense of identity, both positive and negative.

A belief can easily have the ability to limit us. *Limiting beliefs* are opinions, thoughts, and statements of truth that can stop you from achieving your goals.

Examples Of Limiting Beliefs
- "I'm not good enough."
- "I'll never be successful."
- "I don't have enough experience."
- "I'll never be a great leader."

The more we give in to limiting beliefs, the more our sense of who we are is stunted. What is possible is diminished. As the American Author Louise Hay once said, "If you accept a limited belief, then it will become a truth for you."

A belief can limit you, but a belief can also empower you forward. An Empowering Belief is a belief about ourselves that is both positive and helpful. They are called Empowering Beliefs because they quite literally give us the power to become who we were made to be.

Examples Of Empowering Beliefs
o   "I am good enough."
o   "I can and will be successful."
o   "I am able to grow and learn."
o   "I am a leader in the making."

The weight of limiting beliefs can be suffocating. They hold us back from reaching our true potential. What if we decided to shed those beliefs, let go of the chains that bind us, and embrace the limitless possibilities within us? Imagine the power that could be unlocked and the heights we could reach if only we had the courage to break free from the shackles of our limiting beliefs. It takes immense strength and determination, but the rewards are immeasurable.

Your Values - Values are the driving force behind our actions, the compass that guides us through life's journey. They shape our beliefs, decisions, and, ultimately, our destiny. They are the principles you live by. A principle is a fundamental truth or proposition that serves as the backbone of our system of beliefs, behaviors, and chains of reasoning.

They are your core truths guiding you through your decision-making process. Like a cornerstone, your values are the foundation upon which your entire identity is built.

We must hold onto our values with unwavering conviction to truly unlock our inner potential. The better your values, the stronger and more resilient your identity will be. When we stand firm in our values, we stand tallest as individuals.

Good values lead to good behavior, produce good results, and lead to the development of good character. The different types of characters are called virtues.

Example Of Virtues
- Bravery
- Generosity
- Truthfulness
- Friendliness
- Diligence

The more you foster virtuous values, the more confident, secure, and ethically minded you will become. The Roman Emperor Marcus Aurelius said, "The happiness of your life depends upon the quality of your thoughts; therefore, guard accordingly, and take care that you entertain no notions unsuitable to virtue and reasonable nature."

The shining beacon of virtuous values can elevate and empower, but the dark abyss of vices will harm and debilitate. A vice is a malignant value that leads one down the path of self-destruction and corrupts the very essence of one's being. It brings with it chaos and ruin, crushes potential, and shatters self-belief. At all costs, avoid vices. They will lead you nowhere good in a hurry.

Example Of Destructive Vices
- Cowardice
- Stinginess
- Boasting
- Belligerence
- Laziness

As you strive to live a virtuous life, you will find that your self-respect will grow and, with it, your confidence. The more confident you become, the more courageously you will fight yourself. You have the power to take control of your vices and replace them with virtues. In doing so, you will exchange behaviors of self-destruction for behaviors that build you up.

Your Mindset - Growing up in a ghetto in Bulgaria, I was enmeshed in a world that was often hopeless and full of despair. The people around me were resigned to their fate, often believing that their circumstances were set in stone. Starting a business, changing their fortunes, and learning from mistakes were not concepts that existed in their minds. If you were born in the ghetto, it seemed as though that was where you were doomed to stay.

As I began to expose myself to people in the business world, I realized how truly different their mindset was from that of my youth. They believed that nothing in life was fixed and that everything could be changed and improved. Instead of viewing mistakes as prison sentences, they saw mistakes as opportunities to learn and grow. This realization was a turning point in my life.

With this new perspective, I was able to see opportunities where before I could not. My circumstances no longer limited me. I believed that I could change my fate. This mindset shift was the key that unlocked a world of possibilities.

Your mindset is the very foundation of your being, the culmination of all your attitudes, values, and core beliefs. It is the driving force behind every decision, every action, and every thought. It holds the power to shape your reality, to limit you or to set you free.

Having the right mindset is the difference between living a life of mediocrity or one of unparalleled growth and success. In her best-selling book *Mindset: The New Psychology Of Success,* Dr. Carol S. Dweck explains why some people fall apart in the face of challenges while others turn their setbacks into comebacks. She believes that it all comes down to the way a person thinks. Many success factors, such as self-belief, resilience, and the willingness to strive toward excellence, come down to whether a person has a growth or fixed mindset.

Fixed Mindset | According to Dweck, those with a fixed mindset believe that their personal qualities are set in stone and cannot be altered. This belief leads to a lack of motivation to improve oneself and reach their full potential.

Fix Mindset People:
1. **Focus on validation** - Prioritize validation from others and constantly seek validation in order to appear smart and successful.
2. **Seek certainty** - Driven by the need for certainty, often remaining within their comfort zones in order to ensure success.
3. **Pre-judge potential** - Believe that success is solely based on innate talent and abilities. This can result in inflating their own abilities to feed their ego.
4. **Get stuck in a failure cycle** - Label themselves as a failure and give up, often searching for blame or excuses to protect their image.

Growth Mindset | Individuals with a growth mindset believe that through effort and dedication, they can continuously improve and develop. This mentality allows them to embrace challenges, learn from failures, and persevere through obstacles. This leads them to greater success and fulfillment.

Growth Mindset People:
- **Focus on Learning** - Be in constant pursuit of knowledge, actively seeking to expand your horizons and understanding of the world.
- **Seek Challenges** - Embrace challenges as opportunities for growth and learning, pushing yourself to reach new heights.
- **Belief in Ongoing Improvement** - Recognize that personal development is a lifelong journey and actively seek out ways to improve in all areas of life.
- **Learn from Failure** - View mistakes as valuable sources of feedback, and use them to identify areas for improvement and progress.

In order to achieve outer change, we must be willing to re-adjust, re-think, and re-examine our inner beliefs. The more actively you exchange a fixed mindset for a growth mindset, the more your sense of what you can do and achieve will expand and grow.

You Are What You Aim At

Napoleon Hill, the author of *Think and Grow Rich*, says that, "The starting point of all achievement is desire. Keep this constantly in mind. Weak desires bring weak results, just as a small amount of fire makes a small amount of heat." There is great power in knowing what you want. The more you desire it, the more willing you will be to make the changes required to be successful. The more confused you are about your desires, the less likely you are to have the courage to fulfill them.

As an executive coach, I always start my first session with a new client with two simple yet profound questions. Question one is, "What do you hope to achieve? If your life was an arrow, what target are you aiming at?" Almost always, they have an answer. They often tell me about goals like growing their company, improving their marriage, or even losing weight.

After I help them clearly define exactly what they want to achieve and how they believe they can achieve it, I will ask question number two, "Why?" What is inspiring them to take action? Are they doing it for money? For their kids or maybe their wife? Almost always, depending on how they answer this question, I can tell whether they will reach their stated goals or if they will fail.

Why?

Because your WHY matters. It will be your WHY that will push you forward, inspire you to take action, and empower you to push through. The stronger your WHY is, the more likely you will be able to change your habits, critique yourself, and take the hard steps to experience true transformation and achieve the success you want.

Spirit, Soul, & Body Alignment

I have taught for years that the key to unlocking your potential begins with aligning your inner self with your outer purpose. Every individual consists of three domains that make up the self—your spirit, soul, and body. Like stars in a constellation or a solar eclipse, incredible things begin to happen when these three domains are aligned.

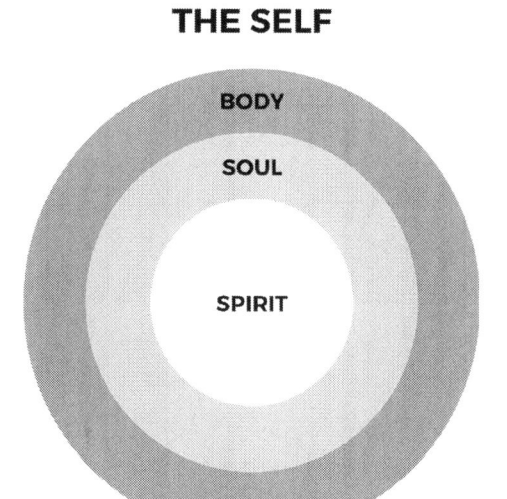

THE SELF

(Diagram: concentric circles labeled BODY, SOUL, SPIRIT from outer to inner)

Your Spirit - Your spirit is your core. It's your connection to the divine–the infinite power and potential of all existence.

Your Soul - Your soul is connected to emotional intelligence. It's the domain of social psychology and social relations to other people.

Your Body - Your body is the material. It's the accumulation of intelligence, talent, and physical capability that you possess.

Several years ago, I was coaching a client who was suffering from panic attacks. He was a high-ranking C-level executive at one of the largest companies in the country, making six figures annually. Roughly halfway through our groundbreaking session, I asked him how he had been coping with the stress of anxiety.

"Alcohol and shopping!" he told me. He would end almost every night with half a dozen drinks and shopping for designer clothes online. In fact, his shopping addiction had gotten so out of hand, he had filled a second apartment with hundreds of thousands of dollars worth of clothes he would never be able to wear.

Knowing full well the man was in desperate need of intervention, I challenged him to pack his car full of new clothes he had bought recently. Instead of ending his night at the bar, he would instead meet me at an undisclosed location with a secret challenge. A few days later, the man arrived to meet me after work. He was shocked when I revealed to him we were standing outside a Goodwill for high school boys. Over the next two hours, the man would give away all of his designer clothes to boys in need. By the end, he was emotionally and completely healed from panic attacks.

I tell this story to illustrate the power of aligning one's body, mind, and soul. The man was experiencing regular panic attacks because his busy schedule caused him to lose sight of what really mattered. He was spending all his time trying to fill the void inside himself with material stuff. What he was really looking for was meaning. Yes, he had achieved professional success. However, the man found himself asking, "What did it mean?" The answer was not more material possessions. What he discovered that day was that his success could bless other people. He aligned His body (the act of giving) with his soul (relationship with boys in need) and his spirit (his inner call to be a light in a dark world). The true measure of success is meaning.

What is true sacrifice worth? If you can answer that question, courage will always come. Why? Because the more you care about what you are fighting for, the more you will do to make it reality.

Live for a Higher Purpose

In the face of great adversity, it's easy to feel like where you are right now is where you will always be or who you are now is who you will be in the future. The truth is that every successful person who has achieved something great *became* that person. They did not start out knowledgeable, skillful, and wise. They learned and perfected their craft through hard work, determination, and *self-belief*. That's the power of identity. It's not just about knowing who you are, but it's also about having the guts to become who you know you could be.

In order to supercharge your journey of identity transformation, here are four helpful steps you can take daily to define your identity.

STEP ONE | Visualize Your Ideal Self

A great way to visualize your future self is by taking the Success Life Area Assessment. After rating each life area on a scale from one to ten, take fifteen minutes and descriptively write out what your ideal life would look like over the next couple of years! Once you do, take five to ten minutes weekly, monthly, or quarterly to review your ideal life and answer these questions:

1. How would you feel?
2. How would your life be different?
3. What opportunities would you have that you don't have now?

STEP TWO | Create an Ideal Self Routine

Before I became a successful pastor, executive coach, and entrepreneur, I would spend every morning as *if* I was a super successful millionaire. I would take a cold shower, drink the best coffee, work out in the morning before work, read the business section of the morning paper, and put on a great outfit. It's amazing how much you can do, experience, and enjoy without millions of dollars.

Over time, my morning routine became the anchor of my day. It would mentally prepare me for what I wanted to achieve the rest of the day and change my mindset from fixed to growth. Why? Because it allowed me to live like my future self in the present. Once I reached my goals, I already knew who I was and how to live as the real me.

STEP THREE | Create Daily Declarations

Shape your identity by creating a set of daily declarations. A declaration is a formal statement of your wishes and desires.

Every morning, before I start my routine, I first recite my daily declarations. By speaking out loud about what I desire for the day, I open myself to what life has to offer. At the end of this chapter, I included my personal list of declarations I repeat every morning. I also created an exercise that will help you write your own. This way, you can actively speak life over yourself every day. I hope it blesses and empowers you.

STEP FOUR | Practice Self-Care

As a Pastor, I want to tell you that you are loved. You are loved by God, who created you. You are loved by many people around you. I also want to tell you how important it is to love yourself and to treat yourself like someone who loves you.

The more you love yourself, the more you will value yourself and believe that you are worth taking care of. If you are a person who struggles with self-love, use the daily declaration exercise at the end of this chapter to breathe life into yourself every day. Actively declare to yourself that you are loved, you are worth it, and that your life is a gift.

Why? Because you deserve it.

CHAPTER 8
PRINCIPLES

Success Principle #1

Break free from your limiting beliefs.

Success Principle #2

Stand firm on your values.

Success Principle #3

Exchange fixed for growth mindset.

Success Principle #4

Align your body, mind, and soul.

Success Principle #5

Create your own daily declarations.

Chapter 8 Exercise
MAKSIM'S DAILY DECLARATIONS

Christ is my center! I exist for Him to be exalted and for the people far from Him to know Him.

Me and my house will serve the Lord. I love my wife and lay down my life for her. Our children grow up in wisdom every day because we teach them the Way they should walk - they will not go stray.

My wisdom and power are Divine, I have creative solutions in every situation.

My intuition is clear, I have divine intelligence and a spiritual understanding of what is, what has been, and what is to come!

I am an instrument of light - my thoughts, words and actions reflect the Glory of God!

Today I am better than yesterday, I wake up with a mission, I have a purpose and I will fulfill my assignment.

My mind is as sharp as a blade, my body is healthy, and my soul is satisfied.

I am conscious of every divine opportunity that comes my way. Not a single blessing will pass me by.

God has given me the power to accumulate wealth, I am a steward of abundance, I saw generously and reap a hundredfold.

I love mankind, I see the best in people and I devote myself to finding the treasure in each person.

I begin where all others give up. I give my best, I am a believer and I never give up.

Today the world will become different, and better due to my ministry because I am in Him and it is no longer I who live, but Christ who lives in me!

*Write down daily declarations that you can speak over your life every day

Chapter 8 Exercise
DAILY DECLARATIONS

Write down daily declarations that you can speak over your life every day

CHAPTER NINE
The Power of Habits

*"We are what we do all the time.
That is why perfection is not an act, but a habit."*
Aristotle

When I first decided to take control of my health, I knew it wouldn't be easy. I also knew that the rewards would be worth it. I joined an exclusive health club near my downtown office and made the commitment to train five days a week and eat a healthier diet.

At first, I was filled with enthusiasm and determination. There were days when I felt unmotivated and sore. I started to doubt my ability to reach my goals. Then, something amazing happened. I was working out with a successful bodybuilder client of mine and I asked him if he always loved working out. He smiled and said, "Of course not. Many days I'd rather stay in bed."

That's when it hit me. Success is not about always feeling motivated or loving every minute of the journey. It's about having the determination to show up and give it your all, no matter how you feel. That's what makes success a habit and separates the amateurs from the professionals.

If you are like most people, there are probably a number of things you would like to change about your life. Maybe you'd like to exercise more often, learn about a new subject, get up earlier in the mornings, or stop smoking. The secret to creating the life you want begins and ends with the habits you are willing to create, change, or even eliminate.

Anatomy of Habits

If you asked me on Monday morning what I'll be doing on Wednesday at noon or Friday night, I would tell you that I'll be making meaningful progress forward in my personal, professional, and family life. How can I be so sure? Because the majority of my behaviors and tasks are habit-based. Every week I take my wife out for date night. Every morning I wake up at the same time, take the same cold shower to wake me up, and declare the same words over my life. I lift weights at the gym and do cardio. When I get into the office, I repeat the same set of work based habits before my first meeting.

One small action might move you forward a little in a day, but targeted, repeated behaviors can produce incredible results. The key is to make those behaviors consistent. Eventually, they will become habits.

Great habits bring success in all areas of life.

A habit is…

an activity, ceremony, observance, practice,
process, or protocol you perform daily.

Some habits are small. We perform them over and over again without realizing it–like the habit of turning on a light when you enter a dark room. All the small actions we perform while moving throughout our day on autopilot are habits.

Habits can also be large. Spending an hour at the gym every morning is a habit. Meeting with your assistant every morning at 9 AM is a habit. Our lives are made up of repeatable protocols, activities, and procedures.

Regardless of the specific protocol you repeat, James Clear explains in *Atomic Habits: An Easy & Proven Way to Build Good Habits & Break Bad Ones*[11] that every habit is comprised of Four Simple Stages:

STAGE ONE | A CUE

A cue is a simple trigger that sets our brain in motion toward performing a behavior.

STAGE TWO | A CRAVING

A craving is the desired change in reality.

STAGE THREE | A RESPONSE

A response is a habit you perform.

STAGE FOUR | A REWARD

A reward is the final benefit of the habit.

Example of Habit Stages:
- *Cue - Your phone rings*
- *Craving - You want to know who's calling you.*
- *Response - You check your phone.*
- *Reward - You connect with a loved one.*

These four stages serve as the framework for every habit. Together, they function as a habit loop that our brain follows each time we perform them. Psychologists at the Massachusetts Institute of Technology discovered in 1999 that habit loops often happen subconsciously. They are created by

---

[11] James Clear, *Atomic Habits: An Easy & Proven Way to Build Good Habits & Break Bad Ones*, (Penguin Random House, 2018), pg 9.

a dopamine feel-good reward system that, through repetition, creates a connection between a trigger and reward within the brain.[12]

Similar to feedback loops in chapter two, habit loops can be desirable or unwanted. A desirable habit is a trigger-response-reward system that produces good results and positive outcomes. Examples of desirable habits include exercising, reading before bed, and drinking a glass of water with meals.

An unwanted habit is a trigger-response-reward system that produces negative outcomes. Examples of unwanted habits include overeating, scrolling through social media, or drinking excessive alcohol with dinner.

Regardless of the unwanted habits you'd like to change, it is possible to harness the power of habits and rewire your brain. There is a proven path to exchange your unwanted habits for desirable ones.

The Great Habit Exchange

When I began my new healthy lifestyle, I was determined to turn it into a success. After four months of not consuming added sugar or desserts, I looked in the mirror on my birthday. I was amazed by what I saw. Not only had I lost 25 pounds, but I also didn't miss the sweets at all! Later that afternoon, I had my first piece of birthday cake in a while. I didn't even finish the slice!

This experience taught me that bad habits can be broken. It's easy when we feel desperate to convince ourselves that things can't change. But nothing could be further from the truth. I also learned that it's much easier to replace a bad habit when you are actively trying to practice new ones. Many times I tried to "stop eating sugar," but I was only successful when my goal was to "start eating healthy."

Every time I won the day by eating healthy, it became a little easier to

---

[12] Stacey McLachlan, *The Science Of Habit*, Healthline, December 21, 2021. https://www.healthline.com/health/the-science-of-habit#8

pass on sugar. After a few months, I didn't crave sugar or enjoy it in the same way I used to. Life has shown me that we can break bad habits and create new, healthy ones with determination and consistency. When we take control of our health, we treat ourselves with the gift of a lifetime. Don't be afraid to dream big. Don't be afraid to work hard to make those dreams a reality. Remember, consistency is key, and the results will follow. You have the power to transform your life. Take the first step and let nothing stop you from achieving your goals.

How To Break Bad Habits

It's vital to take time to actively reflect on what habits you practice that are desirable and unwanted. There are two steps you can use to break your unwanted habits:

STEP ONE | *Identify habits you'd like to change.*
A great way to identify which habits you would like to change is to create a list of your desirable habits and explain in detail how they make you feel and how they impact your life for the better. When you are done, create an identical list of your unwanted habits. After identifying each habit, explain in detail how that specific habit made you feel and how it negatively impacts you.

STEP TWO | *Actively exchange bad habits for habits that will move you forward.*
Once you've identified your undesirable habits, it's time to create new ones. The most effective way to break undesirable habits is to build new ones in their place. That means swapping old triggers for new ones that re-focus and re-tool your existing reward system.

Automate Your Progress

Fundamentally, habits are sets of certain automated processes and actions. They are formed through repetition and are often established over long periods of time. It is generally the case that the hardest habits to break are ones that you have repeated for years. Our toughest problem areas that require the most amount of work are often created by undesirable habits we have allowed to continue the longest.

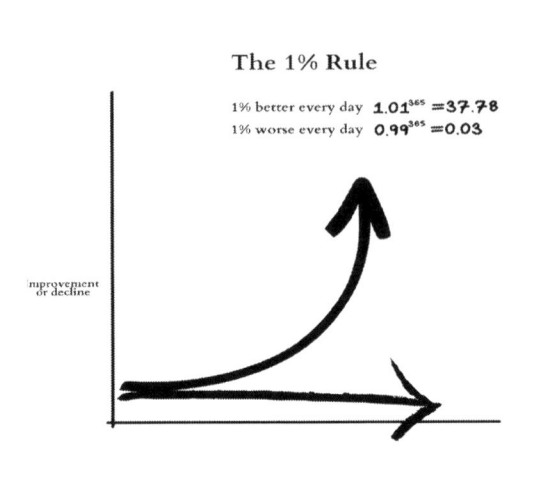

The 1% Rule

1% better every day $1.01^{365} = 37.78$
1% worse every day $0.99^{365} = 0.03$

improvement or decline

On a long enough timeline, even the smallest habits produce large results. In *Atomic Habits*, Clear used the 1% rule to explain how powerful habits create both our successes and failures.

The 1% rule says if you can improve 1% every day for one year, you will see a 37% improvement at the end of the year.

The lessons are extremely powerful. If you can create desirable habits that can make you 1% better every day, week, month, and year, over time, you will have incredible results. Good habits don't just produce good results in the short term. They also produce *great* results in the long term.

Creating Key Habits

A key habit is a daily habit that will propel you toward realizing your vision of long-term success. In this sense, key habits are different for everyone. They will change depending on the specific activity, goal, or area of competency you hope to achieve. For example, if you are a public speaker, your key habits might include practicing vocal exercises before speaking or vocal rest after events. If you're a CEO, key habits can include checking in with your CFO or sales team daily. It can also be working out every morning so you can have the stamina for long hours at work. The difference between a habit and a key habit is that a key habit creates positive results that impact the realization of your long-term goals.

Over time, more of your daily habits can be transformed into key habits. Why? The more you align your daily habits with your long-term goals, the more those routines will become keys that unlock the results you desire.

Developing a Key Habit Strategy

In His bestselling book *The Power Of Habit: Why We Do in Life and Business*, Author Charles Duhigg tells the story of how Michal Phelps, a 23-time Olympic gold medal winner, created his racing day routine that made him a world-class champion. As a child, Phelps was known for being hyperactive and undisciplined. Eventually, when he became a swimmer, he developed a set of key habits that would structure his routine every day for years.

Before Phelps went to bed every night, he practiced a key habit of visualizing a perfect race. Secondly, he woke up every day at 6:30 AM. Thirdly, Phelps began to prepare for each of his races exactly two hours before it began. Lastly, he always performed warm-up laps for exactly forty-five minutes.

Each key habit set the stage for his next habit. By the time of the race, he was ready to perform at his highest level. Some might look at Phelps and say that he became a world champion because of his innate talent as a swimmer. While that might be somewhat true, it's undeniable that Phelps used daily scheduling, rigorous training, and repeatable key habits to help him get there.

That's the power of creating key habits and habit strategies. They set your day in motion and create meaningful progress toward your goals and dreams.

If you want to develop your own key habit strategy, use step one of my Success Journal to begin every day with a life-changing key habit. I promise you that if you can build key habits into your routine, you can automate the meaningful progress you'll need to reach the next stage of where you're headed.

Supercharge Daily Results

Now that you've discovered the power of habits, it's finally time to build your own. Here are four action steps you can use to review your daily habits and build better ones.

STEP ONE | Identity Habit Rewards

Once you've identified a habit you would like to implement, spend a few minutes visualizing how it will affect your daily life. Write down the benefits that your habit will create. Be as specific as possible, especially if the habit you are attempting to implement is difficult.

Published in the Journal of Science, a study by Neuroscientist Michael J Frank at Brown University states that "Dopamine focuses the brain on fixing its attention on the benefits, rather than the drawbacks of completing difficult chores." This is called increasing "cognitive motivation." The better the perceived reward of a habit, the more able you will be to implement the behavior.[13]

STEP TWO | Surround Yourself With Habit Oriented People

Habits are contagious. Numerous studies show that people experience much better results for weight loss, fitness, and sobriety when performing them with other people. The same is true for kids as well. Every parent knows that a child will perform better in school when surrounded by other motivated and well-behaved children. The opposite is also true. School performance can go down if a child finds themselves in the wrong friend group.

The same principle that applies to childhood development also applies to

---

[13] M. J. Frank, Dopamine Promotes Cognitive Effort By Biasing The Benefits Versus Costs of Cognitive Work, Journal Of Science, Vol. 367, NO. 6484, March 2020. https://www.science.org/doi/abs/10.1126/science.aaz5891

team management. A good leader will increase the overall productivity and performance of a team. However, a bad leader can dramatically lower the performance of the same team made up of the same people.

If you are trying to build new habits, take every opportunity to surround yourself with habit-oriented people. If you do, their discipline will become your discipline.

STEP THREE | Live Like Your Future Self

As discussed in the previous chapter, a great way to supercharge your destiny is to live like your dreams already exist. If your dream is to become a millionaire one day, build and perform a millionaire routine every morning. If your goal is to be a champion cyclist or an Ironman winner, build and perform Ironman level habits now as you realize your desired future.

STEP FOUR | Create a Daily Habit Routine

Most of us have a morning routine of some kind. Maybe it's coffee, a cold shower, a daily affirmation, or a morning run. The same happens at work. Maybe it's checking your email, connecting with your assistant, or reviewing your daily to-do list. Are you aware of these habits? Secondly, can they be improved?

When we build our daily habit routine, we can select our morning and work startup habits instead of settling for what we've always done. That's why I created the Key Habit Builder, a guide that will help you review your daily habits and empower you to build ones that produce the results you want.

CHAPTER 9
PRINCIPLES

Success Principle #1

Build great habits to achieve success in all life areas.

Success Principle #2

Let key habits automate meaningful progress.

Success Principle #3

Identify habit rewards.

Success Principle #4

Surround yourself with habit-oriented people.

Success Principle #5

Live like your future self.

Chapter 9 Exercise
EXAMPLE | KEY HABIT BUILDER

What are the key habits and activities you want to stop and start?

	KEY HABITS I WANT TO STOP
1	I will stop eating junk food every night!
2	I will stop watching my favorite TV show every night before going to bed.
3	I will stop getting to bed after midnight.
4	I will not spend more than an hour a day on my social media networks.
5	I will stop drinking more than two cups of coffee a day.

	KEY HABITS I WANT TO START
1	I will start drinking 101 ounces of water a day.
2	I will include fresh fruit into my breakfast every morning!
3	I will read a book 20 minutes a day.
4	I will start waking up at 06:45 so I can go to the gym before work.
5	I will go on a date with my wife every week.

Chapter 9 Exercise
KEY HABIT BUILDER

What are the key habits and activities you want to stop and start?

KEY HABITS I WANT TO STOP	
1	
2	
3	
4	
5	

KEY HABITS I WANT TO START	
1	
2	
3	
4	
5	

CHAPTER TEN
No Turning Back Now

"Better temporary failure than temporary success"
Pythagoras

The path to true success is not always easy, but it is through overcoming challenges and taking calculated risks that we achieve greatness. It is important to remember that even when we attain success, we must not become complacent or take it for granted. History has shown us countless examples of individuals and organizations who have risen to the pinnacle of success, only to fall from grace due to a lack of humility and perseverance.

As we look at athletes who have reached the peak of their careers or powerful business empires that have crumbled, we must remember that true success is not a destination but a journey requiring continuous adaptation and growth.

Let us strive to be humble and always be open for self-improvement. By doing so, we will be able to achieve true and lasting success, in every area of our lives.

Pride Always Comes Before the Fall

The tragic story of the British ship Titanic is one of the most spectacular failures in human history. Most people are familiar with the events that took place on the fateful night of April 14-15, 1912, when the colossal ship collided with an iceberg, suffered a breach, and by morning, sank into the icy waters of the Atlantic Ocean, splitting in two and taking the lives of over 1,500 people.

The Titanic, hailed as an engineering marvel and deemed "unsinkable" by its creators, met a devastating fate in the icy waters of the Atlantic, a cruel twist of irony that will forever be remembered. Built with the ambition to be the largest passenger ship in the world, it symbolized humanity's boundless capabilities, courage, and incredible dreams. But in the end, it became a tragic reminder of how pride will lead to compromised principles that inevitably produce failure.

A lesser-known aspect of the Titanic's sinking is the series of protocol failures made by members of the crew leading up to the fateful voyage. As the Titanic prepared to set sail on its maiden voyage from Southampton to New York in April 1912, a crucial oversight occurred: the key to the binocular locker had been accidentally taken off the ship. This left the binoculars locked away, unable to aid the crew in navigating the dangerous waters ahead. Second officer David Blair had been due to sail with the ship but was replaced at the last minute. In his haste to disembark, he tragically forgot to hand over the key to the binocular locker. The key remained in his pocket, never making the journey on the ill-fated vessel.

As the Titanic tragically collided with an iceberg and sank, taking the lives of 1,522 passengers and crew, an inquiry was held to determine the cause of the disaster. One of the lookouts, Fred Fleet, testified that the binoculars could have saved the ship and the lives lost if they had been available that fateful night. The key to the binocular locker remained in possession of David Blair, passed down to his daughter, a haunting reminder of the role it could have played in preventing one of the greatest tragedies in maritime history.

Even after a century, the story of the Titanic continues to captivate us. We are still searching for answers to how such a promising and ambitious project could meet such a devastating end. The sinking of the Titanic is a cautionary tale, reminding us that even the greatest achievements can be undone by human arrogance and complacency. Even seemingly small decisions to cut corners or slack off can have devastating consequences. Never let pride stop you from practicing the principles that got you to where you are.

A lifestyle of Success

If success is a journey and not a destination, then staying successful is a skill you can develop with dedication and hard work. The road to success is often filled with obstacles and challenges. Here are five important success rules you can live by to safeguard yourself from success sabotage and keep you moving forward with power.

RULE ONE: Prepare For A Marathon And Not A Sprint

As I stepped out onto the football pitch for the first time in a match, I felt my heart pounding in my chest. As I took the field with my teammates, the crowd's roar was an overwhelming experience. I was filled with excitement, and from the sound of the first whistle, I played with maximum effort. I ran with all my might and gave my all with every kick and pass, determined to make a good impression.

But as halftime approached and we retreated to the locker room, my coach pulled me aside with a disappointed look on his face. He told me that he was taking me out of the game. I couldn't believe it. I had thought I had played well, but the coach saw the pain in my eyes and explained that it was because I was tired. This wasn't the practice field we trained on every day of the week. This was a big stadium with a much larger field. There was a reason we had tactics and specific positions.

It was a humbling moment for me, but also a valuable lesson. It's easy to get caught up in the moment and try to do too much, but the truth is that success is not a sprint. It's a marathon. It requires focus, hard work, and perseverance. It's essential to stay focused on the things that matter and adopt the philosophy that success is a journey, not a destination. From that day on, I stayed within my limits, listened to my coach, and focused on the goal. And in the end, it paid off, as I became a better player and a wiser person in the process.

RULE TWO: Change The Way You Speak
Imagine a life where every goal you set for yourself is within reach, where success is not only achievable but guaranteed. It all starts with the words you choose to use.

Think about it. Before any important event or meeting, you probably ask yourself, "What do I have to do to succeed?" You weigh the pros and cons of your actions to calculate the outcome.

What if you could change the way you talk to yourself? What if you could replace words like "impossible" and "I can't" with words that empower and inspire you? The fact is, the words we use shape our reality and determine our level of success.

When was the last time you truly thought about the words you use? Have you taken the time to analyze your inner dialogue? If not, now is the time. Remember, you can't change the world before you change your words.

One of the key differences between those who succeed and those who remain successful is that successful people give themselves grace. They have learned to apply self-denial to their negative qualities and to accept the good in themselves. By changing your vocabulary, you can change your reality. Empower yourself with positive words and watch as success comes naturally. Take control of your inner dialogue and your life.

RULE THREE: Be Grateful, Not Satisfied

True satisfaction cannot be found in material possessions like a bigger car or a bigger house. It is unlocked within you only in those moments when you realize that nothing is a given. It's when you are grateful for the air in your lungs, the blood that flows in your veins, and your heart that works even when you sleep without consciously controlling it. It's when you realize that you have been given so much that you do not deserve that you are grateful for the gift of life. This is when true happiness begins.

The happiest people I know are not always the richest, but they are certainly the most grateful. The Bible speaks of good success. Having good success indicates that bad success exists as well. When you can't appreciate things, no matter how much you have, you don't become happier. On the contrary, you often become busy and worried. That is why it is so important to define success for yourself and realize that being grateful is good success.

In the end, God created you to enjoy creation. In fact, Christ told his disciples, "So far you have not asked for anything in my name, but now I tell you - ask! Whatever is from my Father in heaven in my name, and whatever you ask, believing that you have received it, He will give it to you. To make your joy complete." God welcomes you to approach him with all of your desires.

Let go of the notion that happiness is found in material possessions alone. Instead, strive for a life filled with gratitude, ambition, and a never-ending pursuit of creating meaningful memories. Remember, true success is not measured by what we have but by how we feel and how we impact the lives of others. Be grateful, but never satisfied.

RULE FOUR: Fail Forward

Even if you follow every instruction in this book to the letter, you will inevitably encounter failure. There will be days when you can't stick to your morning routine, moments when you make the wrong decision, or when fear paralyzes you. It's not the failure itself that determines our success. It's our perspective on it.

When we experience failure, it's hard to assess the true extent of the damage to our self-esteem, ego, and soul. It takes time to objectively evaluate the situation and determine where we went wrong and why. It's important to remember that every failure is just another step on the path to success.

Achieving success is not a linear process, and it's important to acknowledge that it will be filled with challenges and setbacks. Just like climbing a mountain, there will be steep and treacherous paths that we must navigate alone. But, when we reach the summit, we will be reminded that our perseverance, endurance, strength, and faith in ourselves are what brought us there.

It may seem contradictory to talk about failure in a book on success, but it's important to prepare for the inevitable and to view it from the right perspective. Remember, nothing in life happens to us, but rather for us and ultimately contributes to our growth and development. Failure is not the opposite of success. It's an essential part of it.

When I embarked on my physical transformation and weight loss journey, I had days where I faltered. There were days when I indulged in unhealthy foods and ate more than I should have. Instead of letting the failure consume me, I took a step back and analyzed the circumstances that led me to make those choices. I quickly got back on track and returned to my diet.

Falling off the wagon is a common experience, but what sets successful people apart is the ability to get back up and continue moving forward. It's important to remember that it's not the number of times you fall that matters but how many times you get back up. You're one step closer to your goal every time you stumble and get back up.

The beauty of failure is that you can fall forward. You can still make progress toward your goal. It's important to embrace and learn from failures. They are a natural part of the process. Only when we accept the possibility of failure can we truly appreciate the journey and all the hard work that goes into it.

RULE FIVE: Do It For Someone Else

Achieving success is not just about reaching personal goals and acquiring material possessions. The most important key to true success is dedicating that success to something greater than oneself. Putting God, your family, and the common good at the center of your ambition guarantees that your success will be long-lasting and fulfilling.

I have observed that those who achieve exceptional levels of success in life are always driven by a higher cause. They strive to have more for their children, their loved ones, and the greater good. This selfless mindset sets them apart from those whose sole purpose is to accumulate more for themselves.

In my life, I have come to believe that almost every significant blessing, whether material, emotional, or spiritual, that I have received was a result of my desire to serve others. This was not karma but rather following the golden rule of doing to others as you wish to be done unto you. Dedicating your life to a cause bigger than yourself ensures that your life leaves a legacy. Your works will be remembered and celebrated and will serve as an inspiration to future generations.

Noteworthy individuals, whose monuments are placed in the heart of every city, whose names bear the central streets and boulevards, schools, and universities, did not achieve their grand deeds through selfishness and ego-centrism. They were inspired to serve something greater.

Let go of the notion that success is solely about accumulating more for yourself. Instead, strive for a life dedicated to a cause greater than yourself. This will not only bring you true success and satisfaction, but it will also ensure that your legacy lives on for generations to come.

Chapter 10 Exercise
YOUR LIFE CHECK-IN

Each of our lives is a sum total of eight interconnected life areas.
Rate yourself from 1-10 in each life area.
Compare your current score to your last score.

SUCCESS LIFE AREAS	SCALE	PREVIOUS SCORE	CURRENT SCORE
CAREER	1-10		
FINANCE	1-10		
HEALTH	1-10		
SPIRITUAL	1-10		
ROMANCE	1-10		
FAMILY	1-10		
ENVIRONMENT	1-10		
PERSONAL GROWTH	1-10		

QUESTIONS:

1. What 1-3 areas you have increased the most in?

2. What 1-3 areas would you like to improve in the next month?

A Final Word

As I approached the end of my studies in Sweden, I couldn't help but feel a sense of trepidation. I was about to embark on the adventure of returning to Bulgaria to build my ministry and business from scratch, but the uncertainty of living in post-communist Bulgaria and the weight of my dreams to change the world loomed heavy.

Despite my success as a speaker, with invitations for engagements both nationally and internationally, I couldn't shake the feeling that this path would be harder than if I had stayed in Sweden and built my life there.

As New Year's Eve 2012 approached, I found myself at a crossroads. I was in a crisis, torn between playing it safe and clinging to the comfortable life I had built in Sweden or pushing for true success and the fulfillment of my dreams. The more I thought about it, the more stressed and uncertain I became.

But as I prayed, I felt a sense of inspiration and excitement growing in my spirit. I knew I had to make a decision, and fast.

And then, something miraculous happened. On New Year's Eve, at the house of a friend, a song played that struck a chord deep within me. As soon as the first notes filled the room, I was overwhelmed by a sense of destiny. It was as if that song was the answer to my prayers, and in that moment, I knew exactly what I had to do. I decided to push the needle and fight for my dreams. And with that, I set out to change the world.

I want to leave my footprints on the sands of time
Know there was something that, something that I left behind
When I leave this world, I'll leave no regrets
Leave something to remember, so they won't forget

I was here, I lived, I loved, I was here
I did, I've done, everything that I wanted
And it was more than I thought it would be
I will leave my mark so everyone will know I was here

As I listened to the lyrics, they hit me like a bolt of lightning, urging me to stay focused and never settle for less. This encounter transported me back to a moment a few years earlier when something similar had occurred.

I was younger then, living without electricity and running water, fighting to survive, working at the open market, and selling whatever I could get my hands on. It was one of those days when I wished I wasn't alive and contemplating suicide. I was lonely, poor, and hurting. As a Christian, I knew I couldn't take my life because it would mean eternal damnation.

In a moment of weakness, I turned to food as a form of self-medication. I tried to suppress my pain, eating the most unhealthy version of a burger in a small, fast-food restaurant, feeling miserable and disgusted by my own thoughts. I wanted to cry, but the tears wouldn't come. That's when I heard a piano melody that gave me the same sense of destiny. The words quickly began to flood my soul with hope. It was a moment that changed my life forever.

The song reminded me that even in the darkest moments of my life, there was hope. Despite how hard things might get, I should never give up on my dreams and aspirations. No matter what obstacles I face, I should always keep fighting and never settle for less than greatness.

The lyrics written and performed by Miro that resonated with me profoundly were "That which has been is what will be, That which is done is what will be done, And there is nothing new under the sun." At that moment, I realized that security was an illusion and that true success is found in meaning, not just achievement.

It was then that I decided to follow my calling, which led me to a different life, a different country, and a better version of myself. I wasn't just living in a dream. I was, in fact, happier. When I felt that same sense of destiny listening to the song in Sweden, just as I had years earlier in that small, fast food restaurant in Bulgaria, I understood that I didn't have to be afraid of failure, but only of not trying. A sense of peace and joy overwhelmed me as I accepted the challenge and said "yes" to a new adventure.

I couldn't have known at the time that thousands of miles away, my wife Teodora was also hearing her calling to come back to Bulgaria and make a difference in the world. The same year I returned from Sweden, she left her mother and home in the UK to pursue her destiny.

Years had passed since that night when I heard that song and the voice of God inside of me. On my 27th birthday, I was surrounded by loved ones at a huge birthday party. On the video screen, people from all over the world, including business people, ministers, friends, coaching clients, influencers, and even Tim Story, thanked me for my impact on their lives. Then, my favorite artist, the singer who had touched my life so many years ago, surprisingly appeared on the stage and sang my favorite song to me as a birthday gift.

The same voice and song that touched me at my lowest point now were the sound of my biggest celebration. At that moment, I saw the fullness of God. By His grace, I had turned my crisis into courage. Not only that, but I also had become great friends with the same singer, Miro, who wrote the song that soothed my aching soul. I had the honor of coaching, baptizing, and helping him with his marriage, life, and family. In his darkest moment, I could return the favor he did for me all those years ago. To this day, we are great friends.

As I reflect on my journey, I can't help but wonder what my life would have looked like if I hadn't acted with courage, if I had settled for less, if I hadn't heard the message of that song and understood that it wasn't a coincidence, it was destiny.

I know for certain that I wouldn't be the man I am today. I wouldn't have the two amazing children I have today, and hundreds of thousands of people wouldn't have been impacted by my life. And you wouldn't be reading these lines.

But I did act with courage, I didn't settle for less, and I heard the message of that song. And it changed everything.

As I conclude our journey together, I urge you to listen to your inner voice. It may lead you to stumble and fall, but it also knows how to get you back on your feet. It may challenge you to rise up and take on a new challenge, but it also knows how to make you successful in the midst of a crisis. And most importantly, it knows how to make your life happier and more meaningful in the long run.

Listen! Do you hear it? What does it say? All you need to do now is follow! One step at a time.

DO YOU WANT MORE?

Scan for the "COURAGE COURSE"

COURAGE IN CRISIS: The Ultimate Guide to Success
Copyright ©2023 Maksim Asenov

Printed in Great Britain
by Amazon